WRITERS AND THEIR WORK

Isobel Armstrong
General Editor

CH00956988

CARYL PHILLIPS

CARYL PHILLIPS

CARYL
PHILLIPS

Helen Thomas

For Zora and Orson, with love

© Copyright 2006 by Helen Thomas

First published in 2006 by Northcote House Publishers Ltd, Horndon, Tavistock, Devon, PL19 9NQ, United Kingdom.
Tel: +44 (0) 1822 810066 Fax: +44 (0) 1822 810034.

British Library Cataloguing-in-Publication Data
A catalogue record for this book is available from the British Library

ISBN 0-7463-1124-9 hardcover
ISBN 0-7463-0956-2 paperback

Typeset by PDQ Typesetting, Newcastle-under-Lyme
Printed and bound in the United Kingdom

Contents

Acknowledgements

I would like to thank the School of English and Drama at Queen Mary College, University of London, for the grant of sabbatical leave during 2001–2 and to the editors at Northcote House.

Biographical Outline

1958   Caryl Phillips born on the island of St Kitts, in the West Indies, and brought to England aged four months. He settled in Leeds, where he lived until 1973.

1976   Commenced studies for a degree in English Literature at Oxford University and became an active committee member of the Oxford University Experimental Theatre Club.

1978   Phillips founded the Observer Oxford Festival of Theatre.

1980   *Strange Fruit* premiered at the Crucible Studio in Sheffield.

1981   Phillips's play *Strange Fruit* published by Amber Lane Press. Phillips is appointed Resident Dramatist at the Factory in London.

1982   *Where There is Darkness* published by Amber Lane Press.

1984   *The Shelter* published by Amber Lane Press.

1985   Phillips's first novel, *The Final Passage*, published by Faber & Faber. *The Wasted Years* published by Methuen.

1986   *A State of Independence* published by Faber & Faber.

1987   *Playing Away* and *The European Tribe* published.

1989   *Higher Ground* published by Viking, a division of the Penguin Group.

1991   *Cambridge* published by the Bloomsbury Publishing Group.

1993   *Crossing the River* published by Bloomsbury.

1997   *The Nature of Blood* and *Extravagant Strangers: A Literature of Belonging* published by Faber & Faber.

2000   *The Atlantic Sound*, a non-fictional work, published by Faber & Faber.

2001   *A New World Order: Selected Essays* published by Secker &
        Warburg.
2003   *A Distant Shore* published by Secker & Warburg.

Caryl Phillips has taught in various universities in Sweden, India,
Ghana, Barbados and the United States. His awards include the
Martin Luther King Memorial Prize (1987), a James Tait Black
Memorial Prize (1987), and a Guggenheim Fellowship (1992). He
currently divides his time between London and New York City.

Abbreviations and References

AS   *The Atlantic Sound* (London: Faber & Faber, 2000)

CR   *Crossing the River* (Basingstoke: Picador, 1993)

ET   *The European Tribe* (London: Faber & Faber, 1987)

NB   *The Nature of Blood* (London: Faber & Faber, 1998)

SF   *Strange Fruit* (Derbyshire: Amber Lane Press, 1981)

SI   *A State of Independence* (London: Faber & Faber, 1999)

The past surges like a mighty river. . . . It empties into the present.
(Caryl Phillips, *The Atlantic Sound*)

1

Time and the Black Diaspora

In his *History of the Dispersion of the Jews; of Modern Egypt; and of other African Nations* (1802), William Mavor established a direct connection between the biblical dispersal of Jews from Egypt and the experiences of dispersal and dispossession of thousands of Africans during the eighteenth-century transatlantic slave trade.[1] Six decades later, in 1868, the Sierra Leoneon doctor James Africanus Horton advanced a similar exegesis in his text *West African Countries and Peoples*, while Edward Wilmot Blyden's *Christianity, Islam and the Negro Race* (1887) described the African's existence within the diaspora as being 'not unlike that of God's ancient people, the Hebrews', yet emphasized their continued condition of servitude: 'The Negro is found in all parts of the world. He has gone across Arabia, Persia and India and China. He has crossed the Atlantic to the western Hemisphere. . . . He is everywhere a familiar object, and he is, everywhere out of Africa, the servant of others.'[2] Published in 1910, Sir Henry Johnston's pioneering study *The Negro in the New World* located the concept of the African diaspora within the context of the atrocities of the Atlantic slave trade, whilst W. E. B. Du Bois's autobiographical work *Dusk of Dawn* (1940) described the pain of segregation experienced by blacks in the new world:

> It is as though one, looking out from a dark cave in a side of an impeding mountain, sees the world passing and speaks to it; speaks courteously and persuasively, showing them how these entombed souls are hindered in their natural movement, expression, and development; and how their loosening from prison would be a matter not simply of courtesy, sympathy and help to them, but aid to all the world. One talks on evenly and logically in this way, but notices that the passing throng does not even turn its head, or if it does, glances curiously and walks on.[3]

At the International Congress of African Historians held in Dar es Salaam in 1965, the term 'African diaspora' was used to discuss the plight of blacks throughout the world, while Martin Kitson and Robert Rotberg's collection of essays *The African Diaspora: Interpretive Essays*, published in 1976, reinforced the validity of the term within a variety of academic disciplines. Likewise, Stuart Schwartz's and Paul Gilroy's influential interrogations of the models of diaspora within the black Atlantic world promoted the distinct dynamism of black Atlantic culture, not only in terms of its transcendence of ethnic and national boundaries, but as a concept that has critiqued and developed our understanding of modernity:

> What was initially felt to be a curse – the curse of homelessness or the curse of enforced exile – gets repossessed. It becomes affirmed and is reconstructed as the basis of a privileged standpoint . . . It also represents a response to the successive displacements, migrations, and journeys (forced and otherwise) which have come to constitute these black cultures' special conditions of existence.[4]

As both a development and a departure from the complex and sometimes contradictory models of the African diaspora, Caryl Phillips's work presents a stimulating engagement with the complexities of dislocation and alienation that emerged as a consequence of the unprecedented trade of slaves between Africa, Europe and America.[5] Much of Phillips's work concentrates upon the intersecting histories of these continents, and responds creatively and critically to the psychological effects of fragmentation, cultural dispersal, racism and economic exploitation. As Phillips states in *The Atlantic Sound*, the idea that those blacks who had been displaced from Africa somehow constituted an extended 'family' was soon established amongst those who had been transported on the first slave ships to set sail from the West African coast: 'The idea was seized upon with a particular enthusiasm by those "overseas" who, upon arriving in the Americas, were suddenly distressed to discover that they were black – or to put it more accurately, that they were not white' (*AS* 113).

In both his fictional and non-fictional explorations of the 'black diaspora', Phillips engages with the reverberations of the slave trade, as well as the racist and colonial ideologies that have informed Western practice from the seventeenth to the twentieth centuries. His work thus develops a historiography in which the concept of 'diaspora' is extended as a means of exploring concepts of 'time', wherein the historical is seen as both synthesized and interacting with the contemporary. For this reason, Phillips employs a variety of disparate and divergent narrative voices that interweave across spatial and temporal zones, within a framework that is both intimately personalized and collective. Moreover, it is the conflict and tension arising between these forces and zones that inspires much of his most searching and perceptive work. As Phillips explores the ways in which 'new' identities are created, destroyed and recreated amidst the psychological effects of alienation, migration and dispossession, his work continues some of the theoretical and liberating ideas of thinkers and critics such as James Horton, Edward Blyden, W. E. B. Du Bois, Martin Robison Delaney, Frantz Fanon, Stuart Hall, Toni Morrison and Paul Gilroy. In an interview with Rosalind Bell in 1991 Phillips explained the ways in which some of the central themes of his work, most especially the effects of racism and the paradoxical pressures of cultural assimilation, interconnect with his own experiences of growing up within the diaspora:

> Immigrants want to forget [their past] because they are so concerned with their kids becoming a part of the new world. They want them to become part of the new society, so they don't want them to remember where they came from. That's really what happened to me. My parents didn't talk about it, and it wasn't something that was taught at school. We weren't reminded that we were West Indian; we were reminded that we were black.[6]

In its exploration of the 'psychic wastelands', and cultural segregation established by the pernicious influence of Western colonial and racial history, Phillips's work endeavours to highlight the transatlantic connections, negotiations and disjunctions between Britain and its colonies.[7] His exposure of such parallels and differences not only works towards a recovery of a past heritage, but also underlines the dynamic interactions between the past and the present. As a consequence, Phillips demonstrates the potential reformulation of such traumatic experiences and crises of the past within the present. In order to expose these agents of cultural interaction, Phillips's narratives

3

promulgate a revised temporal schema that transcends the restrictions of linear time. By juxtaposing the narratives of individuals inhabiting different periods of history, Phillips's work suggests the ways in which 'time', and indeed cultural memory, may be seen as moving backwards into the past, as well as forwards into the future.[8] From this perspective, the importance of the past is reinforced and 'time' itself begins to take on a more expansive dimension of collective experience and, indeed, vision. This 'reorganization' of time as it exists within the diaspora departs from its place and status within the modern Western philosophical and scientific world.

In the ancient world, much of the religious and philosophical debate was concerned with the paradoxical relation between concepts of eternity and transience, historical time and human existence: for the ancients, time was an entity that contained every paradox. In Book II of his *Confessions*, St Augustine of Hippo responded to his own question – 'What, then, is *time?*' – with the enigmatic reply: 'If no one asks me, I know; if I want to explain it to someone who asks me, I do not know.'[9] For Augustine, who died in AD 430, time, like space, emerges from nothing, out of nowhere – in other words, as the 'number of motion with respect of "before" and "after"'. In Book IV of his *Physics*, Aristotle identified time as a 'cosmological fact' hinged upon 'change', while Plato's metaphysics highlighted what he perceived as a clear distinction between the realm of *time* and the realm of *being*. For Plato, time was merely an imperfect 'moving image of Eternity' in which man exists as an imperfect reflection of the *timeless* domain of pure and perfect forms inhabiting the realm of eternity.[10] According to both Plato and Augustine, therefore, the classical divinity of Christianity existed *outside* time, in the perfect realm of eternity, knowing all time, all pasts, presents and futures.[11]

During the seventeenth century, however, following the impact of work by Galileo and Newton, time was redefined by science as a measurable quantity. As suggested by Edmund Hayley's poetic dedication to the third edition of Newton's *Principia* (1726) entitled, 'Ode to this Splendid Ornament of our Time and Our Nation', Newton's *The Principia: Mathematical Principles of Natural Philosophy* (1687), in which he formulated his three famous laws of motion and the theory of universal

4

gravitation, had had a profound impact upon the accepted laws of motion and theory of universal gravitation:

Behold the pattern of the heavens, and the balance of the divine structure:
Heaven has been conquered and its innermost secrets are revealed:
The force that turns the outermost orbs around is no longer hidden
.   .   .   .   .
Now we know what curved path the frightful comets have
.   .   .   .   .
WE learn at last why silvery Phoebe move[s] at an unequal pace.[12]

According to Hayley, Newton's hypotheses about the principles of space and time had achieved a liberation of mankind from the encumbrance of 'error and doubt'. Newton's spatial and temporal theories had provided mankind with the 'secret keys to unlock the obscure earth', enabling him to be 'admitted to the banquet of the gods': 'Join me in singing the praises of NEWTON, who reveals this. . . . No closer to the gods can any mortal rise.'[13] For Hayley, therefore, Newton's ground-breaking text not only demonstrated the ways in which all bodies – terrestrial and celestial – obeyed the same gravitational laws, but had established the calculus required in order to discover and predict the ways in which things worked and moved. 'Motion' was seen to take place in an infinite, immovable space, while time was defined as 'absolute', flowing eternally with perfect uniformity and 'without relation to anything external'. Newton's *Principia* thus distinguished between concepts of space and time in terms of their 'absolute and relative, true and apparent, mathematical and common features'.[14]

The eighteenth century's obsession with achieving greater precision in measuring time was motivated not only by philosophical or scientific considerations, but by practical matters of navigation and trade. By the late eighteenth and early nineteenth centuries, confidence in the 'predictable' nature of time and space had inspired and facilitated an unprecedented level of Western colonial and imperialist activity.[15] While ships criss-crossed the Atlantic in pursuit of wealth and goods from the slave trade, the laws of thermo-dynamics developed by nineteenth-century physicists were used to highlight the perceived 'universal' principles of degeneration. This process, which regarded every closed system as tending towards a state of disorder and chaos, was subsequently linked to ideas of cultural progress and degeneration, history and 'non'-history, as determined by the observations of the German philosopher George Wilhelm Friedrich Hegel about Africa. According to Hegel, whereas the emergence of Christianity in the Western world confirmed the evolution of self-consciousness, spiritual development and individual freedom, Africa was an 'unhistorical continent, with no movement or development of its own'.[16] While Hegel acknowledged that slavery was a moral injustice that contravened the very essence of humanity, he believed that slavery could become an *actual* injustice only if a slave *claimed* his right to be free; a slave who accepted his condition, therefore, was as much to blame as his slave-owners.[17] Echoing Augustine's dilemma in his *Lectures on the Phenomenology of Internal Time Consciousness*, the philosopher and leader of the German phenomenological movement Edmund Husserl (1859–1938) articulated some of the paradoxes and confusion involved in time-consciousness:

> Naturally, we all know what time is; it is the most familiar thing of all. But as soon as we attempt to give an account of time-consciousness, to put objective time and subjective time-consciousness into a proper relationship . . . we get entangled in the most peculiar difficulties, contradictions, and confusions. . . . The consciousness of space . . . belongs in the sphere of what is phenomenologically given . . . something similar is also true of time.[18]

These 'difficulties, contradictions and confusions' arise not only from time's relativistic nature, but also from its slipperiness in terms of definition. L. Feuerbach's essay of 1839, 'Towards a Critique of Hegel's Philosophy', had argued that Hegelian philosophy effectively abolished the 'pastness' of time:

> For Hegel, the 'time present' is eternity. Therefore his method succeeds in abolishing the past *as* past, and the future *as* future. The past is taken up by memory into the actuality of the present and its husk is thrown away as mere 'existence'; while the future is treated as wholly immanent to the rationality of the present of the interpretation.[19]

In its expansion of some of the principle tenets of Hegel's and Feuerbach's analysis, Paul Ricoeur's text *Time and Narrative* presented a version of historical time that rejected the speculative tradition of thinking of time as 'cosmological fact' and placed it within a context that highlighted the temporality of human existence.[20] Ricoeur's subjective, phenomenological approach contradicted models based upon an objective framework of time – that is, as a natural condition exceeding and preceding all constitutive activities of the self – and identified the major failure within Augustine's theory of time in terms of its inability to substitute a psychological conception of time for a cosmological one: 'Where Augustine fails is precisely where he attempts to derive from the distension of the mind alone the very principle of the extension and the measurement of time.'[21] For Ricoeur, the opposition between fictive time and historical time corresponds to the major obligation imposed by the historian – namely, 'the need to conform to the specific connectors acting to reinscribe lived time upon cosmic time'.[22] Removing the constraints of cosmological time, according to Ricoeur, has the advantageous effect of liberating fiction from an inscribed form of historical narrative, thereby enabling it to explore the resources of phenomenological time.

Concepts of time and space configured by the twentieth-century physicist Albert Einstein resulted in the identification of particles of light known as 'quanta', which in turn confirmed the existence of atoms. Einstein's theory of relativity revolutionized previously established models of time and reality, liberating them from the strictures of Newtonian thinking and developing them into subjects in their own right. In Einstein's disturbing and controversial schema, the relativity of *space as well as time* was clearly postulated. Einstein challenged time's status as an unchanging backdrop to nature, describing it instead as a mutable and malleable physical entity. Einstein's theories of quantum physics enabled the calculation of probabilities within the subatomic world, which, in theory, corresponded to the possible release of energies locked up within the mass of nuclei at the heart of the atomic world, and in practice resulted in the devastation caused by the two atomic bombs dropped on Hiroshima and Nagasaki in 1945.[24]

The version of time as it exists within the black diaspora, and that Phillips presents in his work, critiques and counterbalances the linear discourse offered by much of Western history and its metaphysics of progress.[25] Within this dynamic model, linear time, as Hortense Spillers comments, 'dips down into the reservoir of collective experience and repairs the apparent fissure between then and now through the systematic repetition of certain inherited cultural gestures'.[26] In its challenge to the strictly linear concept of time's progression, *memory* takes on an essential, critical role. By enabling certain experiences to be 'stretched' over time, memory endeavours to counteract the tyrannies of cultural erasure instigated by historical genocides such as slavery and the Holocaust. Within the (sub)consciousness of that which is 'past', the fragmentation of memory and the paradoxical vulnerability and pain of such shattered histories are both acknowledged and envisaged as a process of survival.

In order to explore some of the ways in which Phillips's work explicates the effects of psychological and cultural trauma established by the ideology and practice of slavery, aggressive colonial expansionism and racist ideology, I have employed the concept of 'black holes' from the theoretical realm of astrophysics. In their discussion of the interrelationship between quantum theory and cosmological black holes, the renowned scientists Stephen Hawking and Roger Penrose have highlighted some of the intrinsic, entropic characteristics of black holes, notably their ability to lose information from our region of the universe: '[We] should say that these claims are controversial: many people working on quantum gravity . . . would instantly reject the idea that the information about the quantum state of a system could be lost.'[27]

In Hawking's and Penrose's conjecture, black holes constitute a 'region of space time' from which it is not possible to escape. This concept of 'black holes' thus provides an excellent means of visualizing black diasporan historiography, corresponding not only to the ways in which time and space are transformed into a form of 'memory' across the diaspora, but representing the erasure of the black psyche from dominant modes of Western discourse, and corresponding models of progression and development. Moreover, these 'black holes' may be used to represent a spectrum of concurrent affirmation and loss, wherein the coordinates of time and space are not only confused but synonymous with the dynamics and conditions of the black diaspora. In a sense, therefore, such 'black holes' may be used to signify a simultaneous process of loss and recovery, interrogation and interpretation, thereby correspond-ing to the intricate, fragile and sometimes contradictory processes of memory. As with the entropic nature of black holes within the universe, memories are not stored within the brain like a series of 'unchanging photographs', but rather exist as an album of 'temporary constellations' of activity, in which neural circuits exist in a constant excitation of sensory images and semantic data.[28] These memories are not 'static' incidents of the past to be filed away until retracted, but rather active, energetic interactions within the present that contribute a crucial part to our sense of self- and cultural-identity. When any one part of the neural circuit is 'stimulated', entire constellations are activated, both chemically and electrically. Each succeeding recollection or retelling *reinforces* the constellation of images and knowledge that constitutes the memory, thereby 'burning the memory in a little deeper each time'.[29] Revisited, these memories become strengthened and form part of the 'architec-ture' of the brain. In terms of the memories informing the black diaspora, these 'black holes' represent not only the 'wreckage of history', as Benjamin purports, but also its recovery and transformation via visionary, imagined circuits.[30]

Transforming and expanding upon Descartes's renowned comment, 'I think therefore I am', Phillips's work suggests that one can only 'be oneself' because of the interaction of individual and collective 'memories' within the past/present. Thus his work, as I shall argue throughout this book, engages with the concept of the black diaspora as both a historiogra-phical and a psychological schema that maps an alternative 'space-time' dimension of the historical consciousness of a dispersed and dispossessed people across a ceaseless duration of history.[31] Like the black holes within the cosmos, the black diaspora both exists, and does not exist, thus performing symbolically both the spectre of cultural eradication *and* the regenerative celebration of survival amidst a nightmarish landscape of ancient and contemporary racial atrocities. For Phillips, as for Foucault, Hegel and Bunuel, without memory there can be no humanity: 'Life without memory is no life at all . . . our memory is our coherence, our reason, our feeling, even our action. Without it, we are nothing.'[32] Moreover, as Phillips's work indicates, memory constitutes a form of refuge and security: 'Where a man keeps his memories is the place he should call home' (*AS* 93). Memory thus establishes and performs our reality, our lives; our 'present' is invaded and negotiated by the past in the same way as our future is linked to our present. At the same time, however, neither Phillips nor Bunuel is prepared to ignore the idiosyncrasies of memory. While memory provides a necessary starting point for all symbolic activity, it, like symbolic activity itself, is 'continually threatened by lapses, holes, and distortions'.[33]

Taken as a whole, therefore, Phillips's work exposes and engages with these 'black holes' of cultural memory, disintegration and revisionary potential. His work thus inspires an active interrogation of memory and forgetfulness within both a spatial and a temporal dimension. By suggesting the ways in which the inheritors/victims of an ancient diaspora might be 'translated' within a metamorphosis of space/time, Phillips promotes 'freedom' as a physical and psychological entity, intricately informed by a constant state of temporal repetition, replay and recovery in which the shame, suffering and self-contempt of the past are translated across a global space. Phillips's work exposes the ways in which the psychological effects of cultural fragmentation and dispersal may be mapped against scientific, cosmological and psychological concepts of time and memory. In his exploration of the dynamics of the black diaspora, memory's role in challenging the strictly linear concept of time's progression and the tyrannies of amnesia is made paramount. Symbolizing the scars of shattered histories and fragmented forms, these 'black holes' of a diasporan time-scape herald the lineaments of transformative vision and recovery.[34] Within this schema, therefore, shame and self-contempt inform, yet do not dominate the processes of memory and time-consciousness. Phillips's work thus creates a temporal fabric that negotiates both rupture and continuity, articulating the narratives of those who fall, both metaphorically and historically, outside their own time zone. Plunging as it does into the nightmarish landscape of trauma, of mutated forms of racism, persecution, genocide and alienation, Phillips's multilayered narrative prioritizes an imaginative historical excavation of the encoded tensions, complexities and nuances contained within the fertile processes of transculturation.

10

2

Strange Fruit

Babylon will fall.

(*SF* 56)

First published in 1981, Phillips's stage play *Strange Fruit* is set in one of England's inner-city areas during the 1970s and focuses upon the confusion resulting from pressures of post-war cultural assimilation and racial isolation experienced by the protagonist, Errol Marshall, the son of West Indian migrants. Originally staged at the Crucible Theatre in Sheffield in October 1980, Phillips's play marks an important development in the tradition of West Indian and black British plays staged in London, initiated by the 1952 production of Derek Walcott's verse play *Henri Christophe* and Errol John's play *Moon on a Rainbow Shawl*.[1] However, while Phillips expands upon the pressing themes of racism, post-war migration and post-colonial identity explored within these earlier texts, *Strange Fruit* presents an intertextual engagement with contemporary ideology and discourse on both sides of the Atlantic. Thus, as his title suggests, Phillips's text engages with both Billie Holiday's song of the same title and the infamous photograph of a black lynching in the American South:

> Southern trees bear a strange fruit,
> Blood on the leaves and blood at the root,
> Black body swinging in the Southern breeze,
> Strange fruit hanging from the poplar trees.
>
> Pastoral scene of the gallant South,
> The bulging eyes and the twisted mouth,
> Scent of magnolia sweet and fresh,
> And the sudden smell of burning flesh.

11

For the rain to gather, for the wind to suck,
For the sun to rot, for a tree to drop,
Here is a fruit for the crows to pluck,
Here is a strange and bitter crop.[2]

Born the grandchild of a black Virginian slave and a white Irish plantation-owner, Billie Holiday, née Eleanora Fagan Gough (1915–59), sang 'Strange Fruit' (written by Abel Meeropol/Lewis Allen) as both a protest song against the intransigent problem of lynching in the American South, where over 3,000 blacks had been lynched between 1882 and 1968, and a song of political consciousness in a racially segregated world. Produced in 1939, Holiday's song reflected the increasing escalation of white racism and the continuing impoverished economic and political status of American blacks, despite the efforts of civil-rights organizations in America, such as the National Association for the Advancement of Colored People (NAACP) and the National Urban League (NUL). Sung by Holiday to predominately white, middle-class audiences of the Café Society in Greenwich Village, New York, at a time when many American clubs and bars entertained a 'Whites Only' policy, Holiday's song was first recorded on 20 April 1939 at Brunswick World Broadcasting Studios in the sombre key of E flat minor.[3] Although the rhythm was simple, 'Strange Fruit' presented a savage indictment of the hideous, racist lynchings that had swept across the southern American states. Her reference to the 'blood on the leaves' as black bodies swung in the 'southern breeze' starkly juxtaposed the idyllic, pastoral scene of the American dream with the gruesome detail of black lynchings, while ironically echoing the biblical narrative describing the 'fall' and expulsion of mankind from the garden of Paradise. Critical reactions to Holiday's version of 'Strange Fruit' were mixed. In 1944, the jazz writer and reviewer Charles Edward Smith described it as one of the 'most effective' socially conscious songs, while in 1949 the jazz historian Rudi Blesh described it as an 'unconvincing', 'gauzy' piece in which the Negro 'sells out the birthright of his [sic] own great and original art'.[4]

While Holiday's song, which became known as the black 'Marseillaise', exposed the racially motivated persecutions suffered by American blacks in the years following reconstruction, Phillips's play, published four decades later, transfers that gaze onto the experiences of blacks in post-war Britain. Framed, therefore, by a dialogue with Holiday's post-emancipation lament, Phillips's *Strange Fruit* identifies the individual and collective confusions experienced by blacks in a post-colonial rather than post-emancipation world. Thus, while in Holiday's song the lynched blacks constitute a 'strange and bitter crop', in Phillips's text this crop is extended to include the bitterness, persecution and confusion experienced by the 'strange fruit' of the black-British diaspora.

In Act I, Scene i, the Marshall's terraced house on the Elm Park Estate is described as 'not a ghetto' but 'hardly' suburbia (*SF* 7). The living room is cramped and claustrophobic and its main focal points, a cabinet filled with crockery celebrating the Queen's Silver Jubilee and an arrangement of ornamental migrating birds on the wall, provide an ironic comment upon the racism experienced by those post-colonial migrants who have migrated to, yet been rejected by, the 'mother' colony. While Holiday's song had conjured up a tragic scene of racially motivated violence in 1930s America, Phillips's play is situated amid the racial tensions and intolerances of 1970s Britain. During this period of British history, inner-city areas containing a high black population became saturated by a high police presence, while the controversial Special Patrol Groups (SPGs) and Stop and Search (SUS) laws adopted by the police epitomized the growing suspicion felt towards black communities in Britain.[5] However, as a response to such antagonism and as an expansion of the increasingly visible socio-political and civil-rights movements gaining momentum in America, a far more visible black political consciousness began to emerge in Britain. Indeed, as Phillips's play suggests, this developing dialogue between blacks within the USA, the UK and its former colonies helped to encourage and maintain a sense of black, transatlantic consciousness and socio-political agency.

Strange Fruit captures this emerging sense of transglobal black consciousness, yet also exposes its internal schisms and clashes. While the black power movement within the Caribbean and America advocated a belief in, and demand for, equal rights, it performed and masqueraded via a dominant rhetoric of male violence and promiscuous sexuality. In its transition to Britain, not only did it collide with and depart from the radical feminist

13

politics that were developing across the country but it took place amidst the frustrations and disappointments of post-colonial 'liberation'. In Phillips's play, 21-year-old Errol's relatively young mother is described as possessing a 'premature autumnal serenity', finding herself increasingly cut off from her son's ideals and aspirations as he spouts black power clichés and denounces prominent black figures within the media as 'bloody Uncle Toms' (*SF* 12, 19, 23). Disappointed by the fact that he is wasting his university education, Errol's mother dismisses his valorization of the black power movement, describing it as nothing but 'jigaboos and drug addicts talking about Africa' (*SF* 26). Like many young black Britons of the late 1970s and early 1980s, Errol has no job but is extremely critical of those institutional bodies whose brief it is to tackle racism and improve the public profile of blacks within 'multicultural' Britain: 'What do you want me to do? Go to work for the CRE [Committee for Racial Equality]? Join the police? Stand for Parliament? Or perhaps you want me to make a bid for Trevor McDonald's job and spend the whole day talking shit on the television!' (*SF* 26).

According to his mother, Errol's rejection of the processes of black assimilation into British culture achieves nothing except giving 'black people a bad name'. Errol's belief in pan-Africanism – the unity of 'thoughts and ideals of all native peoples of the dark continent' – draws much of its inspiration from the pan-African cultural nationalism (including *negritude* and Black Power) propagated by black activists and political leaders such as W. E. B. Du Bois (1868–1963), Marcus Garvey (1887–1940), Leopold Senghor (1906–2001), Kwame Nkrumah (1909–1972) and Malcolm X (1925–1964).[6] Taken collectively, these radical activists not only highlighted the cultural and political interconnections within the black Atlantic, linking the political and economic struggles of Africa with the struggles of blacks within the Caribbean, America and Britain, but also exposed the racial inequalities within legal, political and economic systems across the globe. At the turn of the century, Du Bois's analysis of 'double consciousness' had underscored the 'two warring ideals' of being both black and American, an analysis that would later influence the development of the Pan-African Movement and the concept of 'third-world consciousness'.[7] Edward W. Blyden's nineteenth-century pan-Africanist demands for the establishment of an independent state of Liberia found an echo in Marcus Garvey's twentieth-century demands for a settlement community of African-Americans in Liberia, as well as his belief in Black Zionism.[8] While Phillips's play draws upon both the emerging and the historical development of racial self-consciousness within the black diaspora, *Strange Fruit* also exposes the internal weaknesses and blind spots contained within such movements and their contrasting ideologies. Errol, for instance, duplicates Marcus Garvey's commitment to capitalism as well as his rejection of interracial relationships without considering the ways in which his ideas perpetuated notions of racial segregation and hierarchy. In contrast to Garvey, Du Bois had propagated ideas based upon racial, social and political equality as well as democratic socialism. Thus, when Errol propagates this 'new black theory of economics' that he believes will take him back to Africa, his mother undercuts his idealism with a harsh reminder of his own family's economic impotence within Britain. Furthermore, echoing the ideas of thinkers such as Frantz Fanon and Antony Appiah, she highlights the fact that 'Africa' is as much an invention of Europe's colonial ideology as the unified black 'front' that her son imagines himself to be part of, as he denies his Europeanized 'self': 'Talk sense, Errol. How the hell are you going to get to Africa, swim? You've got an overdraft the size of the national debt and as long as you sit on your arse talking shit it's going to grow. . . .What are you fighting?. . .You're doing yourself mad, son. You'll have a breakdown' (*SF* 28, 27).

Although his mother begs him to explain what is troubling him, Errol replies, 'N-O-T-H-I-N-G. . .There's nothing the matter with me. I'm my own man. . . .You go ahead and burn yourself up with pointless worry [but] I'm fine. Doing just fine, thanks' (*SF* 24, 25). Unable to force him to confide in her, she criticizes his disrespectful treatment of both his elders, and his white girlfriend, whom he treats 'like dirt' (*SF* 24, 28). Moreover, Errol's mother begins to realize that her best friend, Vernice, another West Indian immigrant who dreams of returning home to the Caribbean – 'Sometime me feel like just packing up me bag an' going home. Pickin' off me mango and drinking me rum' – shares her son's dismissal of and withdrawal from white

15

culture, accusing her of having become too 'white': 'Lemme tell you girl. One day you going have to join the coloured race' (*SF* 30, 14).

Phillips's play, however, steers away from advocating the vision of voluntary black apartheid prescribed by Errol as a viable, or even desirable, option. Instead, his text exposes the degradation involved in Errol's sadistic treatment of his white girlfriend, suggested by the sordid details of the sex scene that takes place in his mother's living room. Unwittingly, therefore, Errol plays out the condition of the black psyche described by Frantz Fanon, whose internalization of the parameters of racial abuse leads him to misread his 'possession' of a white woman as a substitute for his social ostracization, as he underestimates the extent to which racial inequalities have affected him.[9] Indeed, much of Errol's own rhetoric echoes and fuses the language and form of the passionate speeches made by the gifted orator and minister, Malcolm X and the African-American civil-rights leader Martin Luther King, without acknowledging the distinct differences between them. In the march on Washington on 28 August 1963, a march that became synonymous with the Civil Rights Movement, over 250,000 demonstrators and a worldwide television audience heard King deliver his speech of hope and determination, in which he advocated a vision of racial harmony, love and unity between blacks and whites:

> I'm happy to join with you today in what will go down in history as the greatest demonstration for freedom in the history of our nation. . . . 1963 is not an end, but a beginning. . . . So let freedom ring from every hill . . . let freedom reign . . . [then] we will be able to join hands and sing in the words of the old Negro spiritual: 'Free at last. Free at last.'[10]

While in Phillips's play Errol's statements are imbued with the urgency of King's desire for social transformation, he does not share King's hopes of racial harmony, prioritizing instead a vision of economic *independence* from whites developed from Malcolm X's alliance with the Nation of Islam and the black nationalist group known as the Black Panthers.[11] X's message of racial pride transcended electoral politics, envisaging instead the black race as a nation with a cultural history of its own, and calling for a 'black revolution' that would overturn established political and economic systems.[12] According to X, the racial inequality of blacks in the USA was not just a local, but a *global* problem: '[This] problem . . . is not a Negro problem. [It] is a world problem; a problem of humanity. It is not a problem of civil rights but of human rights.'[13] Condemning non-violence as cowardly and hypocritical, X dismissed civil-rights leaders such as Martin Luther King as 'Uncle Toms', adamantly declaring that the acquisition of legal equality for blacks would only develop into some other nightmare.[14] Although Malcolm X propounded a sophisticated critique of capitalism and colonialism, exposing the intricate relationship between economics, politics and race, Phillips's play highlights the contradictions and dilemmas involved in the psychological and economic 'revolutions' proposed by spokespersons such as Malcolm X, King and Carmichael.[15] As Errol repeats their demands for a separate black state disconnected from the manacles of white society – 'Every time you see a white man, think about the devil you're seeing! Think of how it was on your slave foreparent's bloody, sweaty backs that he built this empire that to-day is the richest of all the nations'[16] – Phillips's play critiques the emergent ideas of black consciousness that were transmitted across the Atlantic from America and absorbed by blacks living in England during the late 1960s and early 1970s, most especially the problematics of 'native regressivism' defined by the Martiniquan writer and activist Aimé Césaire, in his *Discourse on Colonialism* (1955).[17] As a result of these diverging aspirations, Errol's aspirations and ideologies are visionary and revolutionary, yet fallible and naive, as he becomes a representative of the young, headstrong Malcolm X, *prior* to the maturation of his more insightful, intellectual ideas. Indeed, while *Strange Fruit* exposes the weaknesses and idiosyncrasies of both King's and Malcolm X's ideas, Phillips's play underscores their essential role in the realization of demands for racial equality and the development of the black consciousness across the globe.

Errol's mother's friend, Vernice, although worried about her own daughter's absenteeism from school, refuses to take the role prescribed by Errol's discourse of black male superiority or indulge in his ideas of global economic reorganization: 'Plan, me arse. Only planning you'll [Errol will] do is where yer all going get your next spliff from' (*SF* 28). However, instead of encouraging an interracial marriage between Errol and Andrea, Vernice exposes her own internal racism by insisting that Errol should marry a black girl, in an effort to maintain the 'purity' of the black race: 'Girl, you think too white . . . Me ain't want no [half] breeds in my family' (*SF* 31).

In Act II, Scene ii the full extent of Errol's brutally racist treatment of his pregnant, white girlfriend, Shelley, is clearly exposed, as is the limitation of his own pan-African discourse. Referring to her as 'Snow White', he ridicules her ignorance of global politics yet in doing so highlights the superficiality and immaturity of his own political understanding as he displays simplistic tokens of pan-Africanism, casually referring to Alvin's shirt as a 'dashiki' and claiming to possess gloves belonging to the Black Panther Huey Newton. Moreover, while he compares himself to Othello, a lascivious 'old black ram' who has defiled a lily-white maiden, he reveals not only his lack of moral responsibility but also his refusal to see himself as a tragic victim (*SF* 36). Although his white audience is comprised solely of his impoverished girlfriend, he indulges in hackneyed, simplistic black-power clichés about the imminent reversal of power and wealth distribution: 'You don't control shit anymore. You don't control the land, the money or the mind. Now you're the tool and we're the craftsmen. . . . Suddenly you're all frightened. . . . We're a beautiful people, a talented, resourceful, strong, dark people, a people just waking up. . . . The chickens are coming to roost. That's all you are to me – a historical phenomena' (*SF* 38–9). Errol's anti-white diatribe concludes not with a vision of a resurgent black consciousness and racial equality, but with an immature vision of both cultural and racial segregation as he denounces racially mixed pop bands. The sexual act that follows is irredeemably sullied by the derogatory phrases Errol chants at his so-called girlfriend – 'I don't need no fucking white woman to dangle on a string to show that I'm free' – but also tragically inscribed by her failure to recognize the absolute racism implicit in his comments (*SF* 44).

Act II, Scene i, the longest section in the play, opens with a conversation between 'mother' and Vernice in the early hours of the morning. Although the scene begins with mother's recollection of her son's comment about the Christian Church being a white man's institution, it continues via a memory of

18

their arrival in England twenty years previously. For both women, such memories are filled with the horrors of their first encounters with racism in Britain – 'Girl, everywhere we turn. "No coloureds here"' – and their shame following their attempts to relieve their poverty by fiddling the social security in order to pay for their children's school uniforms (*SF* 48–9). Saddest of all is Errol's mother's memory of her experience of trying to find employment in Britain: 'I closed my already heavy and swollen eyes and tried to fight back the tears. . . . Perhaps if they saw tears they'd realize I was human. Perhaps not' (*SF* 50). Errol's mother recalls that when she fell asleep on a bus on her way to an interview and missed her stop, the driver called her a 'nigger' and threw her off the bus so as to avoid what he referred to as 'another Notting Hill riot' (*SF* 51) When she asked for directions, a woman spat in her face, the shock of which caused her to vomit, only to realize that it had begun to snow, an event that she had longed to see as a child, having believed that it would be one of the 'happiest moment of her life': 'I was on the right island. I'd been reading the wrong books. Listening to lies' (*SF* 52).

When Errol's brother, Alvin, arrives back from Africa in Act II, Scene ii, sporting a large gold signet ring and gold chain, the brothers greet each other in 'US fashion', with Errol immediately adopting a Rastafarian voice: 'Raasman. Babylon will fall, Give it time' (*SF* 56). For both Vernice and Errol, Alvin appears transformed, bedecked in jewellery, sporting tight trousers and very short cropped hair. But, while Alvin and Errol had previously dreamed of transforming the world with a 'black' form of economics and politics, the former's visit to Africa has exposed the differences that lie between Africa and the West. Alvin in a sense has come to accept the scepticism anticipated by Fanon and others, towards Pan-Africanism. The fact that Errol does not understand the meaning of the term 'Yoruba' and is surprised to find a 'Made in Hong Kong' sticker on the African carving that Alvin gives him highlights the fact that the brothers' understanding of global capitalism and neocolonial politics has been ill informed and naive. In this way, Phillips's play anticipates and makes accessible the critiques of post-colonialism to be found in writings by activists, academics and theorists such as Fanon, Homi Bhabha, Robert Young and Edward Said, yet situates their dilemmas within the realities of contemporary

British society. Errol's weaknesses and prejudices reflect the limitations and failures of many anti-colonial struggles; failures precipitated by unreflective absorption of eurocentric assumptions and underestimations of the intricacies of global economic networks.[18] While anti-colonial struggles in Africa, India and the West Indies had involved an alternative level of agency by colonized people against the conditions in which they lived, the reality of independence had not proved to be as 'liberating' as it had seemed. Even though these newly independent colonies still possessed valuable resources such as cocoa, coffee, diamonds, gold and timber, the markets for such commodities were found to be 'securely tied up in a maze of international financing, marketing and processing arrangements'.[19] Independence from colonial control had not resulted in an unequivocal severance from the power of former colonial masters, nor a simple liberation from the mechanisms of capitalist power. As the Ghanaian leader and economic analyst Kwame Nkrumah confirmed in 1965, neocolonialism merely continued Hobson's account of imperialism's 'economic exploitation' by another means.[20] As foreign capital was used 'for the exploitation rather than for the development of less developed parts of the world', the unequal system of exchange based upon a metropolitan centre's consumption of the resources of the periphery was not only continued, but encouraged.

Thus, whereas Errol had expected Alvin to come back from Africa speaking the 'lingo', he is surprised to learn from Alvin that there is no 'lingo' there, except 'English' (*SF* 62). His comment highlights his critical *under*estimation of the discrete, yet lethal forces of cultural imperialism. Language, just like the needs and desires 'produced' by the multinational corporations and media conglomerates who have infiltrated the infrastructure of post-colonial countries, functions as both a vehicle and a signifier of economic, material and cultural control, in this case, the interest of international capital and the G7 powers.[21] Moreover, in Phillips's play, the strength of the black Atlantic 'family' is questioned, as the brothers are forced to realize that familial loyalties do not always survive the test of distance or time. Thus, when the brothers recall their visit to the West Indies, they remember their shock at realizing that to some extent immigrants cease to exist within the cultural consciousness of the societies from which they have migrated, a realization that is symbolized by the absence of their father's celebrated memory in the West Indies. Alvin admits that he felt like a stranger in a 'strange land' when he visited Africa, the black 'homeland', and Errol is horrified to hear that Alvin has severe doubts about their forthcoming Black Front 'strike', since he fears that striking will only give white employers an excuse for getting 'rid of . . . [their] black bastards' (SF 65). As a consequence, Errol accuses Alvin of turning 'white en route', of donning, in Fanon's terms, a 'white mask' over a black face.[22] Alvin's response to Errol's criticism highlights the disparities between their 'imagined' versions of Africa and its post-colonial realities: 'You know what it's really like, man . . . It's full of all the diseases of decolonization . . . inflation, unemployment, political violence – remember them?' (SF 69). Errol, however, with a reference to Richard Wright's ground-breaking analysis of the African-American's condition published in 1940, Native Son, unsympathetically accuses Alvin of having turned into the 'curious phenomena of the native son' who looks condescendingly at his own people once he has 'crossed the International Dateline' (SF 69).[23] Alvin retorts that even Errol's education within the British educational system fundamentally severs him from the problems of racial apartheid and extreme poverty in Africa: 'You'd better decide how much of you is Biko and how much is B.Sc. (Econ.).' In an uncanny repetition of Malcolm X's rejection of King's vision of interracial harmony, Errol dismisses Alvin's non-racialized agenda as untenable and intolerable: 'I've heard this shit before, on the telly. You're gonna fight for the dispossessed and oppressed of the world, regardless of colour', insisting that a vision that transcends nationality, colour and race is no vision at all (SF 70). Separated by Holiday's song by gender, genre, geography and a period of almost forty years, Phillips's play reveals how 'estranged' some of the 'fruits' of the transatlantic world have become.

21

3

A State of Independence

You may be brothers alright, but you lost for true for you let the
Englishman fuck up your heads.

Mr Carter had nothing to hurry for, he never had, and he never
would.

(*SI* 45, 136)

In his play entitled *Where There is Darkness*, first presented at the
Lyric Theatre, London, in February 1982, Phillips presented his
audience with the plight of a West Indian man on the eve of his
return to his home in the Caribbean after over twenty years'
residence in Britain.[1] Although set in one of London's commuter
suburbs, the story of Albert Williams subtly engaged with
Shakespeare's characterization of the dispossessed Caliban, a
'thing of darkness', in his play *The Tempest*, and Joseph Conrad's
novella of 1899, *Heart of Darkness*. Four years later, in his second
novel, *A State of Independence*, published in 1986, Phillips
developed the protagonist of his earlier play and imbued him
with some of the confusions and ambivalences characteristic of
protagonists within other texts dealing with the paradoxical
conditions of post-coloniality, such as V. S. Naipaul's *The Mimic
Men* (1965).[2] In this text, Naipaul had highlighted some of the
most pressing failures of the emergent 'independent' nation
states, exposing the predicaments faced by those post-colonial
societies whose colonial rulers had been replaced by a self-
interested black elite. The realities of post-colonialism, as depicted
by Naipaul, suggested that such states had entered a condition of
unmoving stasis in which historical temporality existed merely as
a sequence of constant repetition. In contrast to Naipaul's sombre
pessimism, however, Phillips injects a delicate, almost impercep-
tible element of hope into his post-colonial landscape. As

22

suggested by its title, the novel deals with a distinct period of time – that is, the twenty-four hours leading up to the unnamed island's withdrawal from colonial authority, an island that in many ways resembles the small island of St Kitts where Phillips was born. In *A State of Independence*, a once-colonized island optimistically awaits its 'rebirth' as an independent entity. Phillips's text explores the dynamics of transition, not the revolutionary ethos or violence precipitating the post-colonial moment, but its legal and political consequence. *A State of Independence* thus marks a historical moment of liberation, as the inhabitants of the small island embark upon a project of self-determination and reidentification, as they shed their 'infantile' status for a more sophisticated form of self-government. It is a moment, as the narrator comments, in which the wheels of history have been turned in order to produce the dawn of 'the first day of a new era in [this] island's history' (*SI* 154).

Phillips's protagonist, Francis Bertram, is at once both peculiarly naive and profoundly philosophical, a condition that reflects the island's conflicting inheritances, allegiances and resolutions, as it determines to rename 'Mount Misery' 'Mount Freedom', yet retains its colonial name. Indeed, the citation from Marcus Garvey – 'Your country can be no greater than yourselves' – that forms the epigraph to the novel underscores the ways in which the island must find a means of bringing its past into its present, in the same way that Francis must find a way of establishing a balance between the dilemmas, weaknesses and aspirations of his past and present self (*SI* 7). With these juxtapositions, the novel's structure revolves around the dichotomies of vision and blindness, narrow-mindedness and perspective. In one sense, Bertram is a recast of the Homeric figure of Tiresius, the blind guide who perceives the seeds of the state's future contamination and potential purification. Bertram, on his return to the island, is able to identify the manacles of neocolonialism, apathy and mass consumerism that penetrate and control the island's post-colonial existence, yet is unable to accept the changes that have taken place on the island since his departure. On the eve of national independence, therefore, Bertram can 'see' the continued signifiers of poverty, as the hungry children still stand 'trouserless' along the village roadsides and the cane-cutters trudge like condemned persons 'knowing that fate no longer [holds] any mystery for them' (*SI* 17). Even though Bertram is disturbed by this unchanged landscape of poverty, he finds himself out of sequence with the residents' own sense of hopeful optimism. To them, Bertram has become an 'other', a foreigner who has to be retaught the ways of the island: 'One thing you have to remember . . . is that we don't rush things here. You rushing me too much, and I don't like to be rushed. . . . Things do move differently here' (*SI* 16–17). According to the islanders, Bertram has become too much of a European, in other words, 'unpredictable . . . always causing trouble . . . impossible to insure against' (*SI* 151).

On reaching the home of his childhood, Bertram reminisces about the English vicar, Father Daniels, who prepared him for the scholarship examination that was to prove to be his passport from the slums of the once-enslaved plantation island of his birth to the comparative 'freedom' offered by England. From his retrospective position, Bertram realizes that his focus upon the colonial 'motherland' increasingly alienated him from both his own island and his family, most especially his younger brother Dominic.[3] When he returns to the island of his birth, he does so without any degree of self-condemnation or criticism. As a consequence, his lame excuses for not corresponding with his mother during his twenty years' absence are treated with cynicism and contempt, as she accuses him of shameless selfishness and economic naivety: 'So what England teach you? That you must come home with some pounds and set up a business separate from the white man?' (*SI* 51). In his response to her, Bertram dismisses her uneducated ignorance and labels her 'wretched', adding that the only way for blacks to progress is by setting up businesses 'independent' from those of whites (*SI* 51, 53). Bertram's oversimplistic critique of colonial ideology together with his use of the term 'wretchedness' suggest that Phillips is consciously engaging with the ideas presented by the radical psychiatrist and activist Frantz Fanon, whose *Wretched of the Earth* (1961) applied Marxist analysis to the 'colonial problem' and highlighted the role of literature within the process of decolonization: 'Colonialism is not satisfied merely with holding a people in its grip and emptying the native's brain of all form and content. By a kind of perverted logic, it turns to the past of the oppressed people, and distorts, disfigures and destroys it'.[4]

24

It is only when Bertram embarks upon a conversation with Lonnie at the Ocean Front Bar that he begins to understand that the 'state of independence' achieved by the islanders involves a subtle form of complicity with the old colonial powers. Independence from one colonial authority, it seems, has led merely to continued dependence in another guise:

> Owner-trash is still owner-trash, a funeral director and a doctor gone into partnership to open a rum distillery so that they can both have more business, and our finest minds, the lawyers, the doctors, the odd businessman, who all been overseas to study . . . are so bored with how easy it is to make money off the back of the people that they getting drunk for kicks. (*SI* 63)

In some respects, Bertram's sense of feeling 'out of place' in his own land is a consequence of his own making, as even the street children seem to have a better understanding of global consumerism and post-colonial politics than himself: 'I prefer America,' said the boy. 'New York Yankies, Washington Redskins, Michael Jackson . . . The West Indies is a dead place' (*SI* 103). The local hotel has become part of the Hilton Corporation, with its own artificial boating lake, satellite dish, casino and golf course, and the only blacks to be seen inside are those serving the visitors to the island. Likewise, his old friend turned politician, Clayton, boasts about bringing Pan Am and Hollywood to the island, thereby highlighting the island's defection *away* from the UK and *towards* the USA. Bertram's ignorance suggests that he has been living in a solipsistic, cocoon-like environment in which his self-awareness has remained unchanged and underdeveloped, leading him to believe that, after a twenty-year absence, he can just 'pick up where we left off' (*SI* 96). In fact, Bertram has become a stranger to his own people who either mistake him for an international representative or dismiss him as a fruit that has failed to take root once it has fallen from its parental tree (*SI* 144). Only Patsy, his first love, who is also described as 'a picked fruit rotting', accepts Bertram with 'unqualified joy' and endeavours to create a link between the past and the present (*SI* 81, 87).

When Bertram's old friend Jackson agrees to meet him, Bertram is unsure whether Jackson is parodying himself or the colonial authorities, exposing the fact that the newly indepen-

25

dent state merely mimics the original centre of power. Homi Bhabha's analysis in *The Location of Culture* (1994) determines mimicry as a potentially disruptive threat to colonial discourse, a sign of 'double articulation, a complex strategy of reform, regulation and discipline, which "appropriates" the Other as it visualizes its own power'. Self-parody, however, has no place in Jackson's image of himself as a pivotal force in the island's political transformation. While he sees himself as engaging upon 'the work of history', his critics describe the island's self-prostitution 'to anybody with cash' (*SI* 132, 135). Jackson's analysis, however, of Bertram's misalignment with his native culture is extremely astute: 'You have the wrong idea of the island, Bertram. You walking around thinking that nothing has altered, that nothing much is different, yet you can't see what is before your own eyes . . . He [Father Daniels] make you go blind' (*SI* 111). Exasperated by what he perceives as Bertram's 'blindness', Jackson explains that the islanders are living 'State-side now', and that his control of the island is absolute: 'We living under the eagle . . . Your England never do us a damn thing except take, take, take. . . . You don't even study the island as yet to see how things is . . . You want to invest in the place you remember, not the place that is' (*SI* 112–13). According to Jackson, Bertram has 'lost all sense of perspective, describing him as a product of England' and, hence, of the 'wrong material for the modern Caribbean' (*SI* 133, 136, 139).

It is only after his meeting with Jackson that Bertram begins to accept that he has, indeed, been 'unforgivably naïve' (*SI* 137). Bertram's one-time friend, like the black elite described in Césaire's analysis, has become a relentless man of power. Despondent, Bertram confides in Patsy, who interprets Jackson's antagonist behaviour towards him with the latter's previous adolescent jealousies. Whereas Bertram had considered such rivalries as having been necessarily superseded by the needs of the present, 'What is done is done', Patsy explains that, on the island, nothing 'ever truly falls into the past. It's all here in the present for we too small a country to have a past' (*SI* 142).

On the eve of this 'new era in his island's history', therefore, Bertram finds that he is a lost man, 'rootless on his own island', dispossessed by his own people and cynical of his island's pending 'liberation' (*SI* 155). Yet Phillips's novel *resists* a conclusion of absolute pessimism or unrelenting scepticism. While it is true that Bertram's head appears to have been 'filled with confusion', Patsy teaches him that, on the eve of their island's independence, the only trustworthy celebrations to be had are those of a personal, private nature. The tender sex scene between Patsy and Bertram is thus an evocation of a hopeful, yet fragile future. Bertram's developing maturity forces him to acknowledge that his feelings of rootlessness and isolation are symptomatic conditions of post-colonial migrations. Phillips's text thus concludes with a description of Bertram's intense and disturbing vision of his island on the first day of its independence, as he perceives anew the discreet reminders of a 'troubled and bloody history', as represented by the abandoned sugar mills from the previous episode of colonial slavery (*SI* 157). Faced with these historical ruins, Bertram contemplates the means by which he might make peace both with his past and with his island's future. As he watches a man thread wires from telegraph pole to pole, he begins to understand the frustrated predicament of the island. Although the island is now linked 'telegraphically' to the other small islands in the Caribbean, this web of cable connection connects them 'live and direct' to America, reinforcing the fact that the fate of Bertram's native island lies at the hands of international conglomerate media industries. Thus, while Phillips departs from visions of post-coloniality that determine the new nation states as impotent echoes of their former colonizers, his text suggests that such 'states of independence' must find a balance between the impact of transnational capitalism and global electronic media. Bertram's final actions in the novel are measured, touching and mature – 'He spat, walked on, and wondered if . . . he should ask Mrs Sutton how he might help his mother' – as he determines to bring the past and present into a new equilibrium, one in which reparation and forgiveness might take place on both a national and personal scale (*SI* 158).

4

The European Tribe

I grew up riddled with the cultural confusions of being black and British.

(ET 2)

In an interview with Rosalind Bell, Phillips described his polemical, semi-autobiographical, travelogue, *The European Tribe* (1987), as a narrative that 'deals with Europe from a point of view which Europe has never had to deal with' – that is, from the barbarism contained within its version of civilization, its often unquestioned racist ideology and practice. Taking its cue from W. E. B. Du Bois's notion of 'double consciousness' described in *The Philadelphia Negro* (1897) and *The Souls of Black Folk* (1903), in which the black simultaneously sees him or herself 'through the eyes of others' as both an enslaved and/or exploited object, Phillips's text presents a sustained critique of the institutional and psychological racism inherent within European historiography, which Marx, a century earlier, had termed the 'profound hypocrisy and inherent barbarism of bourgeois civilization'.[1] While Fanon's critique of colonial ideology exposed the double standards of Western cultural thought and practice, most especially in terms of its racist humanism, Phillips's text extends Fanon's critique by highlighting the relationship between Western-driven global economics and the ideological bases of racist dynamics, while reaffirming the existence of a cultural consciousness within the black post-colonial diaspora: 'I've seen what Europe can be, I have visited Auschwitz and Dachau. . . . The word "tribe" upset some people. But if it's a word that's applicable to black people and red people and yellow people, it's applicable to white people too. If you deal me that card, I deal it back to you.'[2] While Phillips 'redeals' the racist card back to Europe, reversing the trend of racist epistemological thought and Western socio-economic systems, his text focuses upon one of the oldest and most prominent centres of racist/colonial ideology – that is, Britain. Whereas much post-colonial discourse has centred upon anti-colonial movements in Africa, Asia, and Latin America, Phillips's distinct focus upon Europe, and in particular, Britain, is innovative, as he demands that the historical centre of colonial practice examine its own atrocities and engage in its own self-critique. Citing quotations from Claude McKay's *Banjo* of 1929 – 'You're a lost crowd, you educated Negroes, and you will only find yourself in the roots of your own people'[3] – and Derek Walcott's *Midsummer* – 'Praise had bled my lines white of any more anger, | And snow had inducted me into white fellow-ships | While Calibans howled down the barred streets of an empire'[4] – Phillips suggests that his own fragmented sense of cultural identity was compounded by the impoverished and eurocentric education he received in Britain during the 1970s.

By highlighting the paradoxical fragility *and* permanence of black cultural 'roots'/'routes' within the diaspora, Phillips emphasizes the distance between those assimilated within white culture (like the 'lost' but 'educated' blacks in McKay's text) and those dispossessed 'Calibans' who remain on its outskirts. As he explains in *The European Tribe,* after an education within British culture with an absence of black literary role models, it was not until he travelled to America as an undergraduate that he made the 'discovery' that it was possible for a black person to become, or even sustain a career as, a writer. According to Phillips, this form of cultural exclusion contributed to his growing sense of isolation and estrangement as a black and British citizen. Whereas 1960s Britain had been transformed by a surge of buoyant optimism and liberal cultural freedom,the 1970s in Britain was, by contrast, an era of 'tasteless fashions' that existed merely as a 'long and tedious preparation for the industrial decline and depression of the 1980s' (*ET* 2). Having been brought to the UK aged twelve weeks, Phillips describes himself as one of those 'at the older end of a generation' who eventually found their 'communal voice' in the Notting Hill riots of 1976.[5]

29

In his preface, Phillips describes *The European Tribe* as an autobiographical narrative based upon 'personal experience', a text that he claims is neither academic nor able to survive the rigours of the sociologist's laboratory (*ET*, p. xii). Instead, he defines it as an account of 'thoughts encountered' during a year's travel between Morocco and Moscow, begun originally as an endeavour to determine his own relation to Europe, yet later developed into a more sophisticated critique of Europe's historical perception of the dynamics and 'problems' of immigration. Phillips's text deals with the history of migration within Europe, the forces of colonialism and racism that have inspired such migrations, and the development of Europe's sense of self. Accordingly, Phillips re-examines the central role that immigrants have played in the construction of this powerful entity, and explores various forms of racism that have challenged not only their presence but their historical contribution.

Fortunately for Phillips, his own university education coincided with an increased visibility of black culture, demonstrated by the success of African-American and Caribbean artists such as Stevie Wonder and Bob Marley, and the production and dissemination of popular 'blaxploitation' films such as *Shaft* (1971) directed by Gordon Parks (*ET* 3). As Dick Hebidge has convincingly argued, the increasing prominence of black music in Britain, especially the reggae imported into England during the late 1960s and early 1970s, mobilized 'an undefined aggressiveness' in which the emblems of poverty and immigration were embraced by black (and some white) communities resident within England's depressed inner-city areas.[6] Moreover, as both the Caribbean and the USA experienced a forceful reassessment of African heritage within their own parameters, the cult of Ras Tafari and reggae began to permeate the lives of young black Britons, appearing to offer its 'lost tribe' at once a name and a future. However, while Rastafarianism located black Britons within an almost 'sacred' position on the fringes of dominant white society, its religiously inspired metasystem of politics, hinged upon a vision of 'deliverance' from 'Babylon', remained powerfully ambiguous.[7] In other words, as the music and culture of reggae and Ras Tafari inspired a radicalization of black consciousness within Britain's 'black Harlems', its credo of 'suffering' provided an ambiguous model for social and political action amongst blacks.[8]

Inspired by this socio-religious radicalism, yet simultaneously freed from the 'streets of Babylon' by an offer to study at Oxford, Phillips embarked on a 'grand tour' of Europe and the USA while still an undergraduate. With this visit, Phillips developed a more sophisticated understanding of the dynamics of racism and the historical patterns of migration, most especially the wide-scale transportation of Africans during the transatlantic slave trade. Shortly after his arrival in America, however, Phillips became acutely aware of the extreme level of racism experienced by African-Americans on an everyday basis: within a few hours of arriving in New York he is 'questioned' by police, warned about a Ku Klux Klan rally in Atlanta, and referred to as 'boy' by a woman in a hotel lobby in Alabama. It is only when he 'discovers' the work of African-American authors that the parallels between the experiences of blacks across the Atlantic become apparent. Ralph Ellison's *Invisible Man*, Richard Wright's *Native Son* and Harold Cruse's *The Crisis of the Negro Intellectual* present Phillips with poignant and challenging literary articulations of what he describes as 'the conundrum' of the black experience.[9] Published over three decades before Phillips's visit, Wright's *Blueprint for Negro Writing* (1937) identified what the author considered the 'vision' permeating the work of all black writers: 'It is a question of awareness, of consciousness; it is above all, a question of perspective . . . It is that fixed point in intellectual space where a writer stands to view the struggles, hopes, and sufferings of his people.' One of these struggles, as Ellison's fictional work of 1952, *Invisible Man*, revealed, was directed against the refusal of whites to 'see' and acknowledge the black presence that was among them: 'I am an invisible man . . . invisible, understand, simply because people refuse to see me.'[10] Together with Cruse's examination of the role of the black intellectual in the diaspora, these texts framed and directed the parameters of Phillips's own work, developing his understanding of the problems facing blacks and, in particular, black writers: 'I had finished my reading by moonlight. . . . I felt as if an explosion had happened inside my head' (*ET* 7). While the work of Wright, Ellison and Cruse had articulated the plight of blacks in post-abolition America, Phillips's own critical gaze, as the *European Tribe* reveals, was turned towards the configured 'absence' of blacks in contem-

31

porary British and, indeed, European culture, thus prompting him to re-examine the historical reverberations of the 'triangular' trade.

Phillips's travels to America provide him, therefore, with a more sophisticated understanding of the socio-political position of blacks within Europe. On his return to Britain, he experiences a sense of resentment towards the education system that he believes has discouraged his literary and cultural aspirations: 'This alone seemed to condemn the European Academy which had raised and educated me, and I found myself tediously attempting to question everything that I had ever been taught' (*ET* 9). But his disappointment does not end here – indeed, Phillips's condemnation of the British educational system is expanded into a critique of both historical and contemporary national and international racism. As Phillips's 'grand tour' of Europe initiates a 'coming of age', in which his eyes are opened to the continuing effects of racism and neocolonialism, he begins to realize that the chronic level of poverty and unemployment within the post-colonial world is intricately connected to the 'glamourous telltales of media colonization' (*ET* 14). In Morocco Phillips learns that twenty-five million people live well below the poverty line, that 65 per cent are illiterate and that the regular popular uprisings are brutally suppressed by the kingdom's 200,000 strong armed forces, despite its independence from France in 1956 (*ET* 15). In Gibraltar, Phillips discovers that the fragile point of contact between Europe and Africa, the three-mile peninsular, originally named after the first-century Moor Tariq ibn Zeyad, functions as both a NATO store for nuclear weapons and a highly contested military zone between East and West. Moreover, as its residents 'feed' upon an insatiable diet of British television programmes, newspapers and football coverage, they exhibit a profound sense of colonial schizophrenia, a condition that is fed by a fear of uncontrolled immigration from Spain and Morocco (*ET* 27).

When Phillips visits the black American author James Baldwin at his home in France, he is struck by the iron gates outside the author's home, gates that appear both to imprison and to separate Baldwin from the outside world, isolating both his homosexuality and his ideas of racial integration from

French culture. Having participated in the civil-rights struggle in America and having witnessed the deaths of both Malcolm X and Martin Luther King, Baldwin had returned to France. At the time of his meeting with Phillips in the late 1970s, Baldwin had become involved in legal wrangling of a different kind, involving the publication of his book *The Evidence of Things Not Seen*, an account of the murder of black children in Atlanta between 1979 and 1981.[11] In its correlation of the experiences suffered by Baldwin and, indeed, by Shakespeare's famous tragic black 'hero' Othello, the irony of the chapter's title 'A Black European Success' becomes apparent, as Phillips discusses the ambiguous and vulnerable status of blacks living at the centre of one of the world's wealthiest empires. His analysis in *The European Tribe* thus 'backtracks' to a literary, although historically informed, Shakespearian narrative of racial difference and immigration in sixteenth-century Venice (*ET* 45). Like Baldwin in twentieth-century France, Phillips reads Othello's position in Europe as tenuous – his ascent from slave to revered and contracted soldier means that he exists in a continual state of profound insecurity and psychosis, feeling continually threatened, unsure of the parameters he is working within. Unlike Cassio, who is simply a 'foreigner', Othello is an alien, both socially and culturally. Life for him is a complex game in which he does not understand all the rules (*ET* 47). While he believes that marriage to Desdemona will entrench him more securely within Venetian society, to the Venetian nobility Othello is a sorcerer, a black magician (*ET* 4). Their decision to favour Othello's marriage to Desdemona comes about only because they desperately need his military skills. Under the threat of raging war against the Turks, Othello's usefulness as a tool becomes tantamount, thus reducing the proposed, socially unacceptable, interracial marriage to a matter of secondary importance. Like Baldwin's, Othello's circumstances position him as both an unwanted yet tolerated 'insider' and a dubious black 'traitor' in the fight against the powers of the East. Thus, when Othello finds that his endeavours to achieve equality and acceptance in Venetian society via his marriage have failed, he is ultimately 'lost'. Phillips's choice of citation from Louis T. Achille's *Ryhtmes du monde* of 1949 is extremely important here, especially in its anticipation of Fanon's later analysis of the psychological effects of racism: 'In so far as truly interracial marriage is concerned, one can legitimately wonder to what extent it may not represent for the coloured spouse a kind of subjective consecration to wiping out in himself and his own mind the colour prejudice from which he has suffered so long' (*ET* 45).

Othello is indeed a lonely sufferer; when he realizes that he cannot become suddenly 'white', he begins to forget and deny the status of his own past, dismissing it as others have done. Perceiving himself as a lone entity within Europe's sophisticated system of trade and exploitative colonialism, his memory of his past life begins to deteriorate, thus continuing the process of self- and cultural-eradication begun by the European powers (*ET* 51).

This correlation between Shakespeare's and Baldwin's 'mappings' of blackness are crucial to Phillips's own interrogation of racial migration and cultural assimilation within Europe. In his essay 'Negroes are Anti-Semitic because they're Anti-White' (1969), Baldwin had analysed the status of Jews as having occupied a similar, but not identical, status to those of black slaves and their descendants within Europe. As Phillips comments in *The European Tribe*, the emergence of the ghetto in sixteenth-century Venice provided a prototype for the process of racial segregation and ghettoization within the colonial world (*ET* 52). Windowless in order to isolate it from the rest of the city, this 'original' Jewish ghetto was legally sanctioned by the Venetian State in 1516 in an effort to contain those Jews who had first come to Venice in 1373 fleeing persecution from the mainland. By resituating *Othello* within the context of Italy's treatment of Jews, Phillips's analysis thus endeavours to highlight an overt historical and political correlation between Jews and blacks, claiming that for those on the political right, 'and some in the centre and on the left too, 'the Jew' is still 'Europe's nigger' (*ET* 52). However, while the persecution of Jews in Nazi Germany has become a prominent concern within contemporary European consciousness and, indeed, the subject of numerous films, documentaries and articles, by contrast, the travesties of colonialism, the 'rape of modern Africa' and the horrors of slavery remain ostracized, like Othello himself, from the centre of Western culture and its educational policies and practices (*ET* 54).

While in France, Phillips experiences various examples of the country's shrewd hypocrisy and racism that he sees as culminating in the overtly racist declarations of Mr Le Pen's political party. Within French politics, as in other European countries, election propaganda predictably (and often success-fully) pivots around sensationalist and racist fears about immigration and cultural 'purity', even though such cultures unhesitatingly absorb and 'market' distinctly black fashions in music, style and art. Phillips learns that, according to the French government, the (French) colonial 'departments' of Martinique and Guadaloupe are distinct from, and thus superior to, the Africans in Senegal, Mali and the Congo. Not only is colonial logic as pernicious and as calculated within the 'post-colonial' world as it was during the golden age of Western imperialism, but the division and consequential immobilization of Africa's power within the contemporary global economy continues unchecked. Paradoxically, however, as Phillips notes, without its four million immigrants, the French economy would collapse and the price of labour would double overnight. Europe's perceived 'problem' of immigration figures not so much as a *problem* but as a *historical fact* initiated by the consequences of colonial expansionism, exploitative capitalism and shallow liberalism. Thus in Holland Phillips discovers that such liberal-ism evades the increasing drug, pornographic and racist micro-cultures of Dutch society, while in Germany he is shocked by the distinct historical presence yet simultaneous legal 'absence' of the *Gastarbeiter* (guest workers), the imported immigrant labourers recruited to Germany as part of the rebuilding of the nation after the Second World War. Like the Jews in Venice's sixteenth-century ghetto, these *Gastarbeiter*, as Phillips learns, are dispossessed of any civil rights within Germany: they cannot own businesses, vote or claim social security and they live under the threat of 'legitimate' deportation. Absent from the political fabric and financial economy of contemporary German culture, these *Gastarbeiter* do not officially 'exist' yet continue to inhabit a status generally considered to be a 'problem'.

Moving towards a logical conclusion of this critique of Europe's history of racism, Phillips's text ends with a description of his visit to Auschwitz, the site of mass race genocide. As a translation of the term 'burnt offerings', the Holocaust, according to the Martiniquan historian Aimé Césaire, figured as both a condition and a symptom of the racism at the heart of European ideology and practice.[12] For Phillips, the memory of the Holocaust not only 'transcend[s] the imagination' but highlights the urgent and indispensable role of artists, not only as 'keepers of the past, present and future' but also as the potential liberators of distorted histories. Within this schema, the artist's role corresponds not only to the creativity that emerges from the ashes of the past's tragedies, but also as the 'fires of resistance' within both a conscious and an unconscious realm (*ET* 99). Yet Phillips's text does not end with a complacent celebration of the artist's status or responsibilities; rather, he returns to the original focus of his critique – that is, the paradoxical and volatile history and impact of immigration upon Europe's sense of self and its subsequent pervading ideologies. Britain, as Phillips contends, once the powerful centre of the West's imperial philosophy, now exists merely as a cog within the constructed artifice of the European Union. Moreover, just as it has to learn to collaborate and cooperate with other European and global powers, so too must it learn to accept the consequences of its former transatlantic historical and colonial practices: 'Britain's and western Europe's days of imperialistic glory are history' (*ET* 120). Thus Britain must begin to accept the fact that America, 'the Frankenstein that Europe created', has 'risen from the slab' and evolved to conquer and dominate Europe economically, politically and culturally. With this statement, Phillips echoes and extends both the description of the development of the capitalist global economy found within Marx and Engels' *Communist Manifesto* of 1848, and Fanon's description of the USA, as the new imperialist 'monster': 'Modern industry has established the world-market, for which the discovery of America paved the way. The market has given an immense development to commerce, to navigation, to communication by land.'[13]

As Marx and Engels anticipated, colonial expansionism would succeed in securing an exponential development of capitalism, not only by its acquisition of an increased number of global markets, but via its sophisticated system of exchange and commodity (re)production. Phillips, however, adds another chapter to this earlier thesis on global capitalism and colonial expansion, not only by highlighting the role of Africans and other colonized peoples in this unprecedented transformation of global, social and economic systems, but by critiquing the barbarism contained within the 'civilized' cultures of the West. In this way, Phillips's *European Tribe* advocates socio-historical polemic within a morally fired arena in which Europe is asked to take responsibility for its past deeds. Europe, urges Phillips, must accept that its former slaves and colonized peoples, forced by the migratory patterns that it once initiated, can no longer be considered as immigrants, as they now 'wander freely among the noble of Europe's formerly all-powerful cities' (*ET* 120). Thus he concludes by suggesting that Europe's only chance of taking any positive moral initiative depends upon the development of a cogent sense of history, and, in particular, upon an acknowledgement of the racism that lies at the centre of its being (*ET* 121). For Phillips, this involves an active 'remembering' of the 'black holes' of dispossession and persecution that punctuate the time–space dimension of global historiography, as well as an active (re)memory of the creative contribution that migrants have made to Europe's culture and identity:

> Europe is blinded by her past, and does not understand the high price of her churches, art galleries, and architecture. My presence in Europe is part of that price. . . . The discredited are not immigrants, as 40 per cent of the black population in Britain was born here. . . . Europe's current 'problem' relates directly to the permanence of our presence, not our continued arrival. (*ET* 128, 122–3)

Phillips's 'grand tour ' of Europe, therefore, is thus turned in upon itself, becoming a mirrored reflection of its 'dark', hidden past rather than a sycophantic glorification of its 'cultured' achievements. With this conclusion, Phillips moves away from the analyses of the psychological effects of domination and disempowerment in Du Bois's and Fanon's early work, and moves instead towards a more radical demand for social and political empowerment and self-determination within the diaspora. His text concludes, not with a discussion of the alienating effects of dominant white culture, but with the admonition that Europe must see itself first of all as a construct, and thus 'begin to restructure the tissue of *lies*' that are still being taught and digested in schools and amidst political rhetoric: 'For we, black[s] . . . are an extricable part of this small continent. And Europeans must learn to understand this for themselves, for there are among us few who are here as missionaries' (*ET* 129).

5

Crossing the River

She wondered if freedom was more important than love, and indeed, if love was at all possible without somebody taking it away from her.

(CR)

Extending its geographical reach to both sides of the Atlantic and its chronological spectrum to cover a period of over 250 years, Phillips's novel *Crossing the River* (1993) traces a history of the African diaspora from the moment of contact, instigated by the slave trade, between Africa and Europe in the eighteenth century to the present day. Dedicated to those who 'crossed the river', the novel charts the journeys of three African descendants, two brothers and a sister, as they journey through different epochs and throughout different corners of the triangular trade – Europe, America and Africa – in their efforts to establish new places of settlement across the globe. Phillips's novel articulates the dilemmas faced by Nash Williams, a nineteenth-century black American slave-descendant, who 'returns' to Africa as a missionary, the plight of Martha Randolph, an ex-slave who traverses the American West as pioneer on a wagon trail, and, finally, the experiences of Travis, a black American GI, who finds himself posted to England during the Second World War. Framing these journeys is the tragic lament of the children's father, who sold them into slavery and whose voice opens the novel: 'A desperate foolishness. The crops failed. I sold my children. I remember. I led them my children along weary paths . . . [to] where the tributary stumbles and swims out in all directions to meet the sea' (*CR* 1). As this opening statement suggests, the future of the familial/cultural bloodline is represented metaphorically by the river, which, because of the father's actions, is allowed to disappear almost without trace into a sea of global transactions motivated by the slave trade. *Crossing the River* represents a perceptive engagement with the trope of 'crossing'; the African diaspora is seen to traverse spatial and temporal zones, as it confronts social and cultural boundaries across the chasms of history and geography.

Although Phillips handles his material with integrity and sensitivity, his use of the trope of 'crossing' is not unique. Rather, it continues and extends the metaphors of crossing sung as spirituals by blacks on slave plantations across the Americas ('One more river, and that's the river to cross') in relation to the barriers of racial prejudice and political freedom. In Phillips's text, the act of 'crossing' is not confined to physical or social movement but extends to the concept of movement across time. These 'crossings' take place in numerous dimensions, representing not only an intrinsic fluidity between cultures, but also the transformations involved in the constructions of the 'self'. Accordingly, *Crossing the River* promotes a temporal fabric of the black Atlantic diaspora that conjoins notions of the historical with the contemporary and negotiates a continual sense of rupture and disjuncture across both temporal and spatial interstices.

Racism, as it exists today and as it existed during the epoch of institutionalized slavery, is exposed as a process in which the racialized 'other' is located beyond the parameters of predominant temporal and cultural 'zones'. One of the most effective consequences of the transatlantic slave trade, as Fred D'Aguiar has noted, was the severance of blacks from the 'gravitational clutches' of history.[1] Thus, while the triangular trade offered the possibility of dynamic and creative intercultural 'crossings', it also carried with it the potentially hazardous danger of extrication from history's 'orbit'. The Yoruba proverb that implies that the river that does not know its own source 'will dry up' is employed by Phillips to suggest the ways in which premature severance from familial and/or cultural frameworks has a potentially devastating effect upon the development of the individual's sense of self.

Yet Phillips's novel does not limit itself to the fate of the individual, nor even solely to the fate of African descendants, but extends to a creative analysis of the dynamics of both race and culture, which, like water, are seen as ambiguously fluid and slippery. In this way, Phillips's *Crossing the River* exposes the unfixed nature of both race and culture. His novel takes its title from a section of poetry contained in E. K. Brathwaite's *Masks*, originally published in 1968 and republished in 1973 as part of a trilogy entitled *The Arrivants*. Written shortly after the assassination of the black American activist Malcolm X and the end of the Biafran War, Brathwaite's *Arrivants* recounted the migration of blacks over a thousand-year span, from the collapse of the great empires of Sudan to the present day. Seen by many critics as the most distinctive part of Brathwaite's trilogy, *Masks* presents the poetic narrator's search for the reasons behind his people's dramatic loss of power and resonates with the music and rhythm of African cultures, while reflecting upon the legacy of cultural fragmentation and loss.

In both Phillips's and Brathwaite's work, the need for geographical, chronological and ancestral orientation is made paramount. Although divided by over twenty-five years, both authors advocate the need for communal knowledge and individual self-consciousness, while highlighting the critical interdependence between the past and the present. Moreover, both authors examine the interaction between the individual's quest and the role of memory within the diaspora:

> Jazz has been from the beginning a cry from the heart of the *hurt man, the lonely one.* We hear this in the saxophone and trumpet. But its significance comes not from this alone, but from its collective *blare of protest* and its affirmation of the life and rhythm of the group. We hear this in the bass and drums, piano comping, and in the full ensemble which hints sometimes at *chaos, sometimes at anarchy.* But the chaos is always resolved into order. The social sense retains its grip on anarchy. The individual, *it says, still* has his place within the whole, even if, for now, it is a minor segment of that whole. So the trumpet calls, the ensemble answers, comforts, screams out its tight collective protest against the (white) withholding world.[2]

In Movement IV of Brathwaite's *Masks* the poet metaphorically returns to the scene of his people's humiliation – that is, their compliance with and participation in the atrocities of the slave trade. At this point in the poem, the question 'Do you remember?' not only precipitates a moment of crisis and bewilderment but, as Robert Fraser has noted, exposes the 'dead centre' of the poem.[3] The poet's search for his 'origins', his archaeological dig for the 'navel strings' of Afro-Caribbean culture, results in his spade (also a slang term for a 'black') receiving 'dumbness back | For its echo'.[4] His journey 'back' to his origins ultimately fails, as he finds that the uttermost point of his journey is empty, hollow and silent: 'Beginnings end here | In this ghetto'. While the Ashanti people must acknowledge the fact that they have been destroyed by their own greed and lack of social cohesion, the poet must similarly acknowledge the processes of severance, disjuncture *and* cultural continuity between Africa and the black diaspora in the 'new' world.

Phillips's own 'archaeological dig' into the black 'past' reciprocates Brathwaite but adds new emphases. Like Brathwaite's trilogy, his text explores the sense of guilt and betrayal surrounding Africa's participation in the slave trade and presents its readers with a vivid sense of interaction between the past and present. Yet, by including the voices of the colonialists themselves, articulated via the archives of empire and trade by voyagers and travellers such as Sir Francis Drake, Sir Richard Hawkins, Richard Haklyut and John Newton; and by incorporating the experiences of black females, such as Martha, who loses her daughter and husband to slave auctioneers in the the American South, and Joyce, who a century later has to give up her mixed-race son for adoption, Phillips strategically adds another dimension to the narratives of imperialism, racial migration and war. Instead of simply condemning the African father who sells his children into slavery once his crops have failed – 'I soiled my hands with cold goods in exchange for their own flesh. A shameful intercourse' (*CR* 1) – or the English trader who hopes to provide for his family by the profits made by trading in slaves, or, indeed, Joyce, who hands over her 'coffee-coloured' son for adoption, Phillips's novel sensitively engages in the anxieties and traumas experienced by all, both perpetrators and victims, while never losing sight of the intercultural possibilities that lay dormant within such historical episodes.

'Crossing' is thus associated with the fluidity of movement between cultures – the physical and cultural 'crossings' that involve the construction of 'new' versions of the self and the destruction/erasure of others. Crossing the river that separated the north from the south during the *antebellum* era translated American slaves into 'runaway' but relatively 'free' selves, before immersing them into new forms of 'bondage' and restrictive 'ghettoization'. Likewise, for those blacks who crossed from Sierra Leone into Liberia, or Africa to America, or America back to Africa, such movements involved significant transfers of national and cultural identification. But Phillips's text also extends the concept of cultural crossings to the crossing of timelines. Using a distinct narrative strategy, he reconfigures the diaspora as an intrinsic process of fluidity and multivocal interaction that reconfigures, reshapes and remoulds itself across the dimensions of space and time, while redefining their parameters. By strategically interacting with other texts from the eighteenth, nineteenth and twentieth centuries – such as the letters from the Liberian and Sierra Leoneon settlers – Phillips creates a vibrant sense of cross-cultural intertextuality that traces the ambiguities of the 'self' amidst moments of historical crisis and transformation (*CR* 35). In *Crossing the River*, the African male child who is sold to slave-traders by his father is renamed 'Nash Williams', brought up by his master, Edward Williams, as a Christian and, finally, sent 'back' to the Grain Coast of Africa as a missionary and teacher of 'remarkable gifts' (*CR* 7). However, as his letters to his master reveal, Nash begins to develop contradictory perspectives of both America and Liberia as his political and racial consciousness matures: 'America is, according to my memory, a land of milk and honey, where people are not easily satisfied' (*CR* 11, 21, 25). Nash's awareness of such ambivalence highlights the psychological effects of crossing, the sense of displacement that characterizes the condition of the black diaspora. Indeed, Nash's return to Africa not only exposes him to a hostile climate of malaria, smallpox, torrential rain and native attacks, but also instigates his psychological entrance into a 'no man's land' in which racial divisions are exposed as arbitrary and shifting.

Initially Nash thinks of Edward as a father, indeed, as a father who has 'done more for him' than his natural father by taking him from Africa and removing the 'robes of ignorance which drape the shoulders' of his fellow blacks: 'You were kind enough to take me, a foolish child, from my parents' (*CR* 21). However, as the narrative progresses, Nash's letters begin to expose an element of racial tension and religious uncertainty: 'Father, some emigrants hereabouts, having previously embraced religion and displayed the patience necessary to resist the temptation of the evil one, now dance to the discordant tune of drunkenness. I am, however, happy to report that not only my wife but those of our immediate acquaintance remain steadfast in our beliefs' (*CR* 19–20). Indeed, when the novel begins, Nash has been 'missing' in Liberia for over seven years. As his biological father laments the fact that his son, having been taken from Africa and transported to America, is 'beyond', 'broken off, like limbs from a tree', Edward learns that his 'adopted' son, having returned to Africa, no longer wishes to communicate with him, his former master/father. However, while his guilt-ridden African father feels that he can 'rediscover his lost children . . . [if] he listens closely' to the 'many-tongued voices' that traverse the 250 years of the black diaspora, Nash proclaims that he has become a 'heathen' once more, having rejected the religious beliefs and capitalist values of the western world: 'This missionary work, this process of persuasion, is futile amongst these people' (*CR* 62, 63).

Nash's return to Africa under the auspices of the American Colonization Society (a society formed to effect the repatriation of former black American slaves on the west coast of Africa) closely parallels the return journeys made by many 'real' blacks during the eighteenth and nineteenth centuries as part of British and American repatriation and evangelical schemes: 'The American Colonization Society was sure that benefits would accrue to both nations. America would be removing a cause of increasing social stress, and Africa would be civilized by the return of her descendants, who were now blessed with rational Christian minds' (*CR* 9). Published letters from black British 'resettlers' to Sierra Leone – for example, by ex-slaves such as Philip Quaque, Thomas Petters, David Edmon, Susana Smith, Cato Perkins and Isaac Anderson – indicate the continued level of dependency of black repatriates upon their former colonizers and masters: 'By the paper on which I write, you may easily perceive how short I am of Stationary. . .', 'Please . . . grant us one days allowance of fresh Beef for a Christmas diner. . .', 'Let me hav Som Sope . . . plais I hav bin Sick', 'Things will not go well in the Colony unless the people . . . have justice done them'.[5] In 1766, for example, Philip Quaque, who had been born in 1741 at 'Cape Coast', a town just outside the principal British settlement at Cape Coast Castle, Ghana, returned as a missionary to his own people at Cape Coast Castle, having married a white woman named Catherine Blunt.[6] Quaque, a member of the leading chieftain 'Cudjo' family, had originally travelled to England in 1754 under the sponsorship of the Society for the Propagation of the Gospel in Foreign Parts, aged 13.[7] Like Quaque, Nash travels to Africa and settles in Liberia, where he begins to operate a 'most successful mission school for natives', having married Sally Travis, 'a Christian wife from Georgia' (CR 12).

In his letters to his former master, Nash describes Liberia as the 'beautiful land of his forefathers', a place of freedom and equality within which blacks can enjoy their liberty:

> It is the home of our race, and a country in which industry and perseverance are required to make a man happy and wealthy. Its laws are founded upon justice and equality, and here we may sit under the palm tree and enjoy the same privileges as our white brethren in America. Liberia is the star in the East for the free colored man. It is truly our only home. (CR 18)

However, after the death of his wife and child, and after his various requests to his master for food, provisions and medicine have been left unanswered, Nash expresses his desire to return to America, a request that he makes despite accusations that he has had sexual relations with a native woman and, indeed, fathered her child:

> I have been in Africa a long time and I wish to come home as soon as possible . . . Let me know on what terms I can come back, and if I will be interrupted by white people . . . It is naturally my full intention to return to Liberia . . . Liberia is doing her part in improving human affairs, and stands now tall and proud with other regions of the civilized world. (CR 35–6)

In its praise of Liberia, Nash's letters resemble the work of Edmund Blyden, a black born in 1832 and brought to the United States by an American Presbyterian pastor. In 1852, Blyden emigrated back to Liberia, became a government official and published over 100 political tracts and collections of prose writings.[8] In *Liberia's Offerings* (1862) and *Christianity, Islam and the Negro Race* (1887), Blyden compared the British colony of Sierra Leone to the American colony of Liberia, emphasizing that both colonies, as their nomenclature suggested, had been founded by 'private enterprise' and for 'philanthropic purpose': '*Freetown* is the Saxon name for the idea for which *Liberia* is the Latin. Both were given up by their original founders, one after twenty-five years of supervision, the other after twenty-seven years.'[9]

In his letter of October 1840, however, Nash reveals that he has not only married a 'native' woman but has bestowed onto her 'the office of mother to a child' he possesses 'by another, less successful connection' (*CR* 38, 40). Unsurprisingly, and as he admits in this letter, his domestic arrangements have 'caused some offence to those who would hold on to America as a beacon of civilization' (*CR* 38, 40). Not only has Nash resorted to a 'native style of living' while in Africa, but he finds that many of his former 'American fellows . . . privately mock African civilization' (*CR* 41). The question that he repeats, 'Are we not in Africa?' thus reinforces his sense of withdrawal from American, and, indeed, Christian values and beliefs, a severance that is confirmed by his developing understanding of America's hypocritical practice of continuing its slave-trading practices at the same time as promoting black repatriation and missionary schemes:

> Hardly a week passes on this coast of Africa without some report of a sea-bound slaver, and its unfortunate cargo, who have been afforded protection by the unfurling of the Star Spangled Banner . . . To most colored men, who reside here in liberty, and would expect liberty to encompass all of Africa . . . this American protectionism is a disgrace to our dignity, and a stain on the name of our country. (*CR* 41)

Indeed, by claiming his allegiance to Liberia, and not America, as both 'his' country and the 'land of his forefathers', Nash heralds his severance from his former master, Edward, Christianity and Western ideology: 'Christianity . . . in its purest and least diluted form, can never take root in this country. Its young shoots will wither and die . . . I must suspend my faith and therefore freely choose to live the life of an African . . . My faith in you is evident' (*CR* 62–3). In this sense, Nash evokes Edmund Blyden's 1887 disapproval of European missionary practice in Africa and his assertion that Christianity had become too 'Aryan' to suit the black race:

> Owing to the vicious ideas which entered into our training in captivity, and which we are unfortunately transmitting to our children . . . we [blacks] remain in isolation, in poverty, in obscurity . . . because, though citizens of a free, sovereign and independent state we are slaves to foreign ideas. . . . Liberia cannot be a free, sovereign and independent state when her religious development is limited to the views of a foreign race thousands of miles away. . . . The Liberian government has no right to ally itself with the church . . . when that church is not the expression of the life of the people . . . Christianity [must be] forced to retire.[10]

Blyden had read the 'simple and artless but impressive letters' sent from Liberia by early black settlers to their friends and benefactors in America and, adopting Arnold's conception of epoch, envisaged the transatlantic slave trade as the degradation of the sixth epoch. His radical breakthrough, however, was to envisage Liberia as a prototype of anti-colonial struggles that might lead to African national independence: *'We look too much to foreigners, and are dazzled . . . Teach me rather to forget.'*.[11]

Edward's subsequent search for his 'prodigal son', Nash, is thus doomed from the start, and he begins to experience the same dimension of guilt and regret that haunts Nash's own biological father:

> That he [Edward] had banished, not only Nash, but many of his other slaves, to this inhospitable and heathen corner of the world disturbed [him] . . . Perhaps, thought Edward, this business of encouraging men to engage with a past and a history that are truly not their own is after all, ill-judged . . . It occurred to him that perhaps the fever, the sleepless nights, the complex welter of emotions that he had been subjected to since his arrival in Africa, were nothing more complex than manifestations of a profound guilt. (*CR* 52)

In Section II of *Crossing the River*, Phillips describes the plight of Martha Randolph, who, having been sold as a child alongside her two brothers, had worked as a slave in Virginia. She is then separated from her daughter, Eliza Mae, when her master dies and his possessions are auctioned off – the event being narrated in the continuous present tense, in order to demonstrate the trauma of memory that pervades her consciousness:

47

The auctioneer slaps his gavel against a block of wood. I fall to my knees and take Eliza Mae in my arms. I did not suckle this child at the breast, nor did I cradle her in my arms. . . . to see her taken away from me . . . My Eliza Mae holds on to me, but it will be to no avail. . . . 'Moma'. Eliza Mae whispers the word over and over again, as though this were the only word she possessed. This one word. This word only. (*CR* 77)

Sold to a 'deeply religious' old couple, who take her with them to Kansas, Martha 'continues to hear voices' (*CR* 77). When they tell her of their plans to take her 'back across the river' in order to sell her, she, refusing to go back across the 'river to hell', runs away, and becomes a fugitive slave. Phillips narrates this 'passage', from slave to escaped fugitive slave in the call-and-response style of black sermons and song, thereby suggesting that, although 'alone', Martha remains connected with a shared memory and experience that resonates across the black diaspora:

The dark night spread before her, and behind the drifting clods she knew the sky was heavy with stars. (Feeling good.) And then Martha heard the barking dogs, and she tumbled into a ditch. . . . She waited but heard nothing, only silence. (Thank you.) . . . Martha climbed to her feet and began to run. (Like the wind, girl.) Never again would she stand on an auction block. (Never.) Never again would she be renamed. (Never.) Never again would she belong to anybody. (No sir, never . . . Don't nobody own me now.) (*CR* 80–1)

In a precarious place inhabited by blacks, and appropriately named 'Dodge', Martha sets up a new life with a man named Chester. During her ten years there, 'war came and war went' and she discovers a sense of contentment, 'not on account of no emancipation proclamation, but on account of my Chester' (*CR* 84). However, when Chester is shot dead by three gamblers, Martha, an elderly woman by now, joins part of the black exodus that heads west, across prairie and desert, on their way to California, her 'lost' child, Eliza Mae, continually occupying her mind. Six weeks later, unable to cook their food or walk with them, she is abandoned, and, dreaming of her Eliza Mae, dies a lonely, cold death.

Section III of *Crossing the River* demonstrates the ways in which Phillips's text intersects and interweaves with 'other' narratives and manuscripts of empire and slave practice, such as the travelogues and autobiographies published by English slave-traders and adventurers.[12] By means of journal entries and letters, Phillips's text forms a creative dialogue with the work of John Newton, a slave-trader born in London in 1725 who travelled to the West Indies as part of an extremely profitable slave-trading expedition. Published in 1764, Newton's *Journal of a Slave Trader* callously described his five years in the slave trade as an 'easy and creditable way of life'. Similarly his published *Letters to a Wife* (1793) described Africans as being incapable of any emotions or devotions associated with love:

> The creatures [the Africans] . . . are deceived and harassed, by necromancy, magic, and all the train of superstition that fear, combined with ignorance, can produce in the human mind. . . . As for love . . . for the most part . . . to tell them of the inexpressible, and peculiar attraction, between kindred minds; the pains of absence, the pleasures of remeeting, and all the other endearments . . . would be better lost; like describing the rainbow, to a man born blind.[13]

Phillips's fictionalized version of John Newton in *Crossing the River* takes the form of Captain Hamilton, who sets sail on the *Duke of York* for the Windward Coast on 24 April 1752 in order to return with a cargo of slaves:

> *Tuesday 13th October* . . . Saw land, Sierra Leone eastward about 3 miles . . .
> Wednesday 14th October Fair weather. Made a trip with the yawl for water. Visited on board with Captain Williams [Edward Williams's father?] of the *Mary*. He informed me that the *Devon* of Bristol was recently run ashore by the slaves in an insurrection and totally lost.
> *Tuesday 15th October* . . . Corrected the Carpenter with a dozen stripes of the cat for making a commotion while fetching wood . . .
> *Tuesday 25th March* . . . . An epidemical sickness . . . is ravaging amongst the slaves . . . One . . . jumped overboard (No. 97) . . . 2 girl slaves . . . died. Nos 117 and 127 . . . Put overboard a boy, No. 29, being very bad with a violent body flux. (CR 102, 115–16).

Continuing his exploration of concepts of freedom and love, Phillips uses this section of his text to expose the ways in which Hamilton/Newton fail to recognize the paradox involved in their endeavours to establish (and provide financial security for) their families while jeopardizing the lives and hopes of thousands of others (CR 101). Despite the hundreds of African slaves on board his ship, there are few references to them in Hamilton's ledger, except for brief entries about slave prices, suppressed insurrections, high mortality rates and the 'melancholy lamentations' sung by those blacks who huddle together on board his ship (*CR* 103-4). The Africans' existence is objectified and suppressed within his journal in the same way that his complicity with and participation in the slave trade become sanitized and repressed within his own mind: 'My Dearest . . . The lives of the people who dwell hereabouts . . . are petty concerns when set against my love for you . . . My sole pleasure is to dream of our future children, and our family life together' (*CR* 108, 110). However, that experience, which appears to have been successfully repressed and contained within Hamilton's mind, returns over and over again, to traumatize the children's African father who endlessly (re)envisages the moment of separation: 'A desperate foolishness. The crops failed. I sold my children. A shameful intercourse. . . . And soon after, the chorus of a common memory began to haunt me' (*CR* 1). The memory that haunts him, however, is not just that of his own family's disintegration, but the 'common memory' of dispersal and dispossession that characterizes the African diaspora.

The final section of *Crossing the River*, entitled 'Somewhere in England', brings the concept of temporal 'crossings' up to date, unsettling the dust and secrets, the sexual violence, physical abuse, unwanted pregnancies and hysteria, that inhabited the intimate spaces of Britain during the latter part of the twentieth century. In this final section, we witness not the violent dynamics of the slave trade, but the traumatic effects of war in Europe:

> [December 1940] When I saw the town, I wanted to cry. Tram lines twisted like liquorice . . . And in the streets, men with flat caps and women with headscarves scavenged at the ruins of their houses, avoiding the hot debris, trying to find bits of furniture, photographs, anything that remained of their lives.

> [September 1939]. When we got back the evacuees had arrived . . . Before us stood a dozen frightened children, the farmers eyeing the husky lads, the girls and scrawny boys close to tears. . . . Somebody whispered that all of these children wet the bed. That half the mattresses in England were awash, and that at eight and

six per child it wasn't really worth it. I looked across at Len, who firmly shock his head. Not even one of them he said. They can bloody well go back to where they come from. We're not a charity business. (*CR* 179, 144)

The narrative structure framing Phillips's work becomes clear, as both the Holocaust and the slave trade are seen to be premissed upon cultural intolerance and institutionalized violence. In this concluding section of the novel, we encounter Joyce, who records in her diary the devastating effects of war and its aftermath on the women of a Yorkshire community. However, whereas Hamilton's ledger entries in the previous section had appeared in chronological order, covering a period of ten months from August 1752 to May 1753, Joyce's entries appear in non-chronological order, covering twenty-seven years from 1936 to 1963. The period 1936–42 traces her doomed marriage to Len, her mother's death and Britain's engagement in the Second World War; the period June 1942–May 1945 focuses upon the consequences of her interracial relationship with Travis. It is during this period that Joyce is told by an American army officer that American blacks are 'not used to being treated as equals' (*CR* 145). However, she is attracted by the resonance of their voices, and their ways of singing –'that sing-song accent of his . . . the way he stretched out words' – a comment that continues Hamilton's observation of the African slaves' melancholy lamentations on board the slave ships (*CR* 202).

> I turned up my collar and got ready to carry on with my walk. And then I heard their voices starting up. I knew it was them for nobody else in this village sings that way. Like they mean it. I forgot all about the trees and winter. I found myself staring . . . and listening to the sound of their voices . . . Across the road I saw old man Williams . . . He stood and listened as though, like me, he too hadn't heard anything like this before. Just the two of us listening. (*CR* 146)

When Joyce's frustrated husband begins to beat her, 'working off the embarrassment of not having a uniform . . . playing at being a man' (*CR* 159) and is later sent to prison for trading rationed goods on the black market, Joyce shocks the rest of the village by asking Travis to dance at one of the army camp's dances: 'Over his shoulder I could see everyone looking on . . . They were shocked. And maybe a little jealous, but I didn't care

... Looks like you've started the party. You oughta be proud of yourself. I didn't say anything ... I just listened. Listened to him and listened to the music . . . Inside I was smiling' (CR 163). However, Joyce discovers that, after a date with her to the cinema, Travis was violently beaten up by racist army colleagues, who subsequently reported him as having been found drunk and disorderly. It is at this point that Joyce begins to understand a little more about racial prejudice and segregation, as Travis explains that the army only tolerates blacks for the menial jobs they are made to perform.

In July 1944, Joyce discovers that she is pregnant with Travis's child, marries Travis during his seventy-two hours' compassionate leave and gives birth to Greer, their son, alone (CR 218). However, it is only in the closing pages of the novel that we are made aware that, a month before the end of the war, Joyce receives a telegram informing her of Travis's death. This revelation is carefully interwoven with the 'diary entries' of 1963, which narrate the return of her son, Greer, after eighteen years' of separation: '1963: It was nearly four o'clock. I stared at Greer and longed for him to stay as dearly as I longed for him to leave ... A handsome man ... No longer a baby ... I wanted to hug him. I wanted him to know that I did have feelings for him. Both then and now. He was my son. Our son' (CR 224). Joyce's loss, of her lover, to a 'bullet that rips [through] his flesh', and then of her young son to a County Council's children's home, 'the lady with blue coat and maroon scarf', and her subsequent trauma, echo those of Martha and the African father in the preceding chapters. However, although Joyce's section ends with a tragic sense of loss and guilt, it also emits a sense of hope as her 'coffee-coloured' baby returns to see her, voluntarily: 'I knew it was him. I knew that one day he would come looking ... My God, he was handsome. Come in. Come in . . . Sit down. Please, sit down' (CR 223–4).

Phillips's novel thus concludes with a suggestion that, although 'hurt', the children of the African diaspora *will* survive the hardships of their crossings as they arrive on the 'far-bank'. In spite of their fragmented lives and narratives, the life beat of the diaspora, like the 'drum beating on the far bank of the river' will be 'borne in the wind' across the water, traversing both time and place: 'I wait. And then listen as the many-tongued chorus of the common memory begins to swell, and insist that I acknowledge greetings from those who lever pints in the pubs in London . . . the barefoot boy in Sao Paulo . . . the child in Santo Domingo . . . Survivors all' (*CR* 223–4). Reflecting the songs of the slaves and the speeches of Martin Luther King, the haunting chorus of the children's father in the closing pages of *Crossing the River* is intertwined with the voices of Nash, Martha, Joyce and Travis, and resonates with the refrains of black music, jazz and blues:

> For two hundred and fifty years I have listened. To voices in the streets of Charleston. . . . To reggae rhythms of rebellion and revolution . . . I have listened. To the saxophone player . . . in Stockholm. A long way from home. For two hundred and fifty years I have listened. To my Nash. My Martha. My Travis. To the haunting voices. Mercy, Mercy Me. . . . Declaring: Brother and Friends . . . Singing: Baby, baby. Where did our love go? . . . I have listened to the voice that cried: I have a dream that one day on the red hills of Georgia, the sons of former slaves and the sons of former slave-owners will be able to sit down together at the table of brotherhood . . . A many-tongued chorus continues to swell . . . Only if they panic will they break their wrists . . . A guilty father. Always listening. A desperate foolishness. The crops failed. I sold my beloved children . . . But they arrived on the far bank of the river, loved. (*CR* 236–7)

Phillips's concluding passage highlights the ways in which black culture reflects the survival of its members and their dreams, while offering a form of visionary potential: 'Survivors. In their diasporan souls a dream like steel' (*CR* 236). Connecting past with present and future, the rhythms of black music and culture fuse with the language of the written word to present a witness, a testimony to the traumas and liberations of the black diaspora. As these final pages mimic the improvisation of jazz and the call-and-response format characteristic of black culture, the synthesis of personal release and communal action is recreated within a vibrant, 'talking chorus'. Phillips's novel successfully combines autobiographical narrative, political polemic and spiritual chorus to produce a complex cultural fabric. Performance and improvization, chord and discord collide and synthesize within a narrative form that echoes the constant trans-temporal metamorphosis of the black diaspora itself.[14]

6

The Nature of Blood

[The survivor's] suffering is deeply connected to memory. To move
on is to forget. To forget is a crime. How can they both remember
and move on?

(NB 157)

In his ground-breaking and seminal text *The Souls of Black Folk*,
first published in 1903, the African-American W. E. B. Du Bois
made the following statement: 'I sit with Shakespeare and he
winces not.'[1] Three years earlier, at the first organized Pan-
African Association Conference held in London in 1900, Du Bois
had declared that the 'problem of the twentieth century is the
problem of the colour line', thus highlighting the comparable
situations of Africans both within Africa and its diaspora and
encouraging international contact between activists in America,
the Caribbean and Africa. In his novel *The Nature of Blood*,
published in 1997, Phillips engages with Du Bois's comments
and embarks upon a creative interaction between the charis-
matic and mercurial writing of William Shakespeare and the
analysis of the unconscious mechanisms of racism and colonialism propounded by the Algerian psychiatrist Frantz Fanon.
Hence, in *The Nature of Blood*, the psychoanalytically inspired
observations of Fanon are used to read Shakespeare's *Othello*
(1602–4), a play that in turn had been inspired by Girladi
Cinthio's collection of Italian stories *Hecatommithi*, published in
Venice in 1566. Seen in dialogue, Phillips's, Fanon's and
Shakespeare's texts articulate a sensitive evocation of the
'neurotic's predicament' under the conditions of racism and
his overwhelming desire to become 'suddenly white'.[2]

Inspired by the lines in Billie Holiday's song, 'Blood on the
leaves . . . blood at the root', Phillips's earlier play, *Strange Fruit*,

had explored and criticized the limitations of 'negritude', a movement of the late 1960s and 1970s that had endeavoured to reaffirm the place of African culture within the context of other historical intellectual and cultural struggles within the diaspora. In *The Nature of Blood* Phillips tackles the question of race and humanism in a more detailed and expansive way, engaging in an archaeological excavation of a literary and cultural past that endeavours to make sense of the present. Phillips's text takes on three very distinct perspectives. First, it highlights the role of race in both ancient and contemporary (inter)national politics. Secondly, it explores the concept of diaspora as a historical and psychological phenomenon that links both Jews and blacks in their experience of racial persecution and involuntary migration. Thirdly, the novel underscores the psychological effects of diaspora, especially the role of trauma and memory, within the collective consciousness, peripatetic condition and corresponding myths of Babylonian captivity, which function as key components within diasporic narratives of exile and return.

In his radical and innovative text of 1961 *The Wretched of the Earth*, Fanon had highlighted the limitations of essentialist movements such as *negritude*, a term coined by Fanon's Martiniquan teacher, Aimé Césaire, author of *Discourse on Colonialism* (1955) and *Cahier d'un retour au pays natal* (1939), and the concept of pan-Africanism, as promoted by activists such as Tiyo Soga and Marcus Garvey in the 1960s and 1970s:

> The Negroes in Chicago only resemble the Nigerians or the Tanganiyikans in so far as they were all defined in relation to whites. Negro-ism . . . finds its first limitation in the phenomena which take account of the formation of the historical character of men. . . . The problems which kept Richard Wright or Langston Hughes on the alert were fundamentally different from those which might confront Leopold Senghor or Jomo Kenyatta.[3]

Whereas *negritude* had developed in the context of anti-colonialism and African nationalism, the language of African-American nationalism instigated and maintained a political radicalism founded upon demands for equal civil and political rights. However, as Fanon pointed out, negritude in turn promoted a form of 'anti-racist racism' hinged upon retrograde ideas of essentialism rather than cultural synthesis, a *return* to the customs and philosophies of an 'ancient Negro civilization' rather than their development within the 'new' world.[4]

Phillips's *Nature of Blood* discreetly maps sexual and national anxiety onto the dynamics of race. The narrative's framework is established by the voices of the two central protagonists, that of 'Othello' from Shakespeare's Venetian play, and that of a young Jewish woman, called Eva, a character moulded from Phillips's reading of Anne Frank's autobiography.[5] Described by Phillips as a 'sad black man', Othello is first in a long line of 'so-called [black] ancestors' whom he describes as being 'too weak' to yoke their past with their present' (*ET* 45, 54). Although he is a renowned African general hired by the Doge to command the Venetian armies, Othello allows the struggles and dilemmas of his present status in Venice to overshadow the memory of his African past, thereby contributing to an erasure of both his culture's sense of collective historical consciousness and the foundations of his *own* sense of self. According to the omniscient narrator, Othello ignores the Yoruba warning that 'the river that does not know its own source will dry up', and therefore his endeavour to exist without a past ultimately fails:

> My friend, an African river bears no resemblance to a Venetian canal. Only the strangest spirit can hold both together. Only the most powerful heart can endure the pulse of two such disparate life forces. After a protracted struggle most men will eventually relinquish one in favour of the other. . . . While you still have the time jump from [Desdemona's] bed and fly away home. . . . No good can come of your foreign adventure. (*NB* 183)

Othello, to use the words of Richard Wright, becomes an 'ex-coloured man' as he tries to 'forget' his blackness and encourage a surplus of identities, including those that figure him as a complicit witness against himself. In spite of his stature as a renowned soldier and powerful orator, Othello remains a stranger within seventeenth-century Venetian culture; he has no intimates and is the only black man in the play. Thus, while Othello has been summoned to 'serve the [Venetian] state' and 'stand at the very centre of the empire', he still sees himself as a 'foreigner', continually suspecting that 'some plot has been hatched' against him (*NB* 106). In Venice he is confused, unsure whether those around him view him with scorn, contempt or mere curiosity as 'if he were a child' (*NB* 119). While he thinks momentarily of his past life, 'O, I remembered. I remembered', the people around him seem solely concerned with the 'narrow orbit' of their own lives (*NB* 122). Unlike Eva's Uncle Stephan in contemporary Europe, who continually thinks about the family he has abandoned in his own native country, Othello reminisces only very occasionally about his own past. This 'mirroring' of lives and experiences across time is central to Phillips's examination of the psychological effects of cross-cultural migration. Furthermore, the trope of 'mirroring' exposes the ways in which Othello emulates those around him, thus posing a threat to his own sense of self: 'I looked upon myself in the mirror. It was true. The wooing of this lady did indeed threaten the very foundations upon which my life was constructed . . . I abandoned the mirror and made my way to the door. . . . Was I truly the same man?' (*NB* 144–5). Unfortunately, Othello does not consider the similarities between his own condition and those of the Jews, who, like him, have been ostracized from the socio-political centre of the Venetian community. Thus, when he visits the ghetto in Venice, he is astonished to find Jews, rich and poor, living together like cattle in 'one defenceless pen', bound only by their faith (*NB* 130).

Unlike the biblical figure, Moses, who, according to the Old Testament, led his people out of Egypt into new lands, Othello travels alone, into a version of humanity that correlates culture with 'whiteness'. As a consequence, he chooses to erase himself among and for the sake of strangers, thereby entering a 'black hole' of existence in which both his past and his present self are denied. According to Iago, therefore, Othello is the 'lusty Moor' who exists within an 'unhoused' and thus diasporic homeless 'free condition'.[6] Othello has to discover that, within the Western narrative of progress and civilization, his 'blackness' functions as a signifier of *non*-whiteness; hence the tragic inference of his line, 'I am black'. He is trapped, not only by the white man's myth of the black man that produces and repeats images of black lasciviousness, but by his own self-betrayal.[7] Seeing himself as 'without those soft parts of conversation', Othello figures himself as bereft of the signifiers of culture and, therefore, as a commodified object of value.[8] In order to prove his 'whiteness' he embarks on a projectile of abstinence, choosing 'not to please [his] appetite, nor to comply with heat' until it becomes socially acceptable to do so.[9]

In his revolutionary text of 1952 *Black Skin, White Masks*, Fanon turned his attentions not to the objective historical conditions of colonialism, but to the 'human attitudes' inspiring and maintaining those conditions – that is, the cultural and psychological effects of colonialism within the subjective realm.[10] Three decades earlier, in 1928, the black American author and playwright Zora Neale Hurston responded to the question 'How does it feel be colored?' by explaining that she had become 'coloured' when, aged 13, she had travelled from Eatonville to Jacksonville: 'I feel most colored when I am thrown up against a sharp white background.'[11] Similarly, in 1903, Du Bois's *Souls of Black Folk* had articulated the predicament of 'blackness' in a 'white world' by responding to the question 'How does it feel to be a problem?', with an analysis of what he termed the condition of 'double consciousness' – that is, the *doubling* of the black's perspective, the confusing and contradictory condition of being forced to perceive oneself simultaneously as both object and (inferior) subject. By investigating the inner effects of political impotence and racist prejudice (in particular, colonialism), Fanon developed not only a theoretical and psychological model of disempowerment but its counterpart: effective psychological and political activism.

In Fanon's text the central figure is the colonial Negro who is obliged, within the colonial dynamic, to 'give a performance of self which is both scripted by the colonizer and the self', hence producing the internally divided condition of 'absolute depersonalization'.[12] Within this framework, the black's sense of self is fragmented and shattered, and in its place there arises a 'historical schema' that endeavours to weave him out of the 'anecdotes, stories, and anthropological fragmentary details that have been put together by another self'.[13] One of the most powerful of these anecdotal narratives is that of the black's transgressive 'unhoused' sexuality, which, as Othello finds, prohibits his entry into the realms of Venetian society.[14] In order to counteract this entropic system of erasure, the 'negro', insisted Fanon, must place himself not only within his own frame of reference (black to black) but also *in relation* to the white man. The problem with which Fanon was preoccupied was the fact that the black self could exist in relation to himself only *through* the alienating presence of the white 'other', an image that corresponds to Othello's self-imaging of himself as being at once a Turk and a Venetian:

> And say besides that in Aleppo once
> Where a malignant and a turbaned Turk
> Beat a Venetian and traduced the state,
> I took by the throat the circumcized dog
> And smote him – thus.   [He stabs himself]
>
> (V. ii. 360–5)

As Stuart Hall has meticulously argued, Fanon's analysis exposed the inner landscapes of the colonial relation and proposed the elements necessary for the production of a new kind of subject and a decolonized mentality, necessary for the decolonization of the world: 'I propose nothing short of the liberation of the man of mentality *from himself*'.[15] By highlighting the ways in which subjectivity and representation are constitutive of the politics of decolonization, Fanon's critique interrogated the mechanisms of fixed racial signification, explicating the need for new subjectivities if the 'revolutionary' moments of national liberation were to be achieved and maintained. Othello's psychological 'decolonization', however, falls short of Fanon's criteria. While he understands that his marriage to Desdemona will 'mark him off from his past', making him a target of both 'rejection and scorn', he does not fully understand the extent of his own vulnerability, neither in terms of his isolation from his past nor in terms of his own consumption of the colonialist's narrative (*NB* 148).

In *The Nature of Blood*, therefore, Phillips is interested in looking at history from 'a different angle', through the 'prism of a people who have nominally been written out' of history or who have been viewed as the 'losers or victims in a particular historical storm'.[16] Indeed, Phillips's Othello highlights the devastating effect of his self-alienation, as he cries out despondently, 'There is nobody with whom I might share memories of a common past . . . There is no turning back. . . . Let the storm do its work!' (*NB* 160). In order to warn and in some ways counter the effects of historical amnesia, Phillips's text is preoccupied with the sufferings and confusions of those whose lives have been 'undocumented' – that is, those who have faced the cataclysmic waves of migration and persecution that have in turn shaped the nature of the societies in which we live. The novel thus creates a mercurial narrative that twists and turns through different strands of historical and cultural racism, intertwining and juxtaposing the narrative of the troubled Othello in seventeenth-century Italy with that of the young Jewish woman, Eva, as she grows up amidst the hatred and persecution suffered by Jews during the Holocaust. Othello's and Eva's narratives are connected, not only within philosophical models of the Jewish and black Atlantic diaspora, but in terms of their critique of the vagaries and ambiguities involved in the endless production of concepts of *identification*, difference and social acceptance.[17] As a symptom of this process, the signing of the peace treaty between Israel and Egypt in 1979, which created the cross-border zone known as 'Palestine', gave rise to new sites of contention within and around the Egyptian Jewish community.[18] By mapping this dilemma back to that of seventeenth-century Venice, Phillips's text exposes the precariousness of definitions based upon race, 'sameness' and difference, and his focus upon the 'nature of blood' forms a critique of Western humanist ideology in which concepts of the 'self' are constructed both *in relation to* and via the *destruction of* others.

Within *The Nature of Blood* the tentative, yet hopeful, questions of a young boy in a 'displaced persons' refugee camp in modern-day Cyprus revolve around the creation of the new nation state of Israel: 'Our country lay beyond this sand, beyond the black silk of the night sea, away to the south, away to the east. Distant, yet so tantalisingly close, our troubled land. Palestine. Israel. The boy whispered the new word to himself, weighing it carefully on his tongue . . . until he was happy with its presence' (*NB* 3). For the young boy, Moshe, Israel offers the hope of an alternative resting place for the 30,000 'displaced and dispossessed' refugees who have fled the genocide of the Jews by the Nazis. With this opening Phillips reinforces one of the main preoccupations of his novel – that is, the problems intrinsic to the creation of new nation states within a postcolonial, post-Holocaust context. For Moshe, the new nation state is something that can only be imagined – like the biblical promised land, it exists solely in the subconscious realm, an 'imaginary homeland', yet it is essential to his survival.[19] Later on in the text, Eva similarly comments upon psychological definitions of home/ homelands, suggesting that the term 'home' can be used only for a place in which one feels welcome (NB 37). Indeed, Eva's comment reinforces the notion that 'home' must be imagined as a place in which both the past and the present are 'welcomed' in unison. For this reason, she tries to strike a balance between her father's denial of his own impoverished past, as he tries to lose himself in his medical work and pretends that nothing 'untoward' is happening 'at home' in Germany, and her mother's incessant talk of the future they might have in America: 'And then, of course, it was too late' (NB 15, 21).

To some extent, although Phillips wants to celebrate the liberating, radical agency of diaspora in terms of dynamic fluidity, he resists idealizing its potential, seeing it rather as a 'double-edged' witness of the traumatic and transformative epochs of mass migration. The benefits gained from cultural mixing and boundary crossings have to be seen against a traumatic and historical backdrop of slavery, colonialism and racial persecution, as well as ideologies promoting capitalism and dichotomized versions of 'culture' in which the barbaric is seen as a simplistic antithesis of the 'civilized'. In the refugee camp in Cyprus, guarded in military style by the British army, 'idleness' eats away at the refugees' minds, while at night their thoughts wander around an abysmal precipice of horrific nightmares, haunted by the spectre of the Holocaust. Yet Moshe, as Phillips reminds us, is part of a 'new world that is just beginning', a survivor of the old world whose 'new country [lies] hidden beyond the dark horizon' (NB 9). For Eva's uncle, Stephan, however, this 'new home among the Arabs' is still infiltrated and overshadowed by a past he is 'incapable of surrendering': 'Imagine. I still carry with me the old world that I had once cast aside . . . A world that I can never put down to rest' (NB 11). As readers we begin to understand that the old world, which he had to forgo, included his two nieces, Eva and Margot. For Stephan, who encourages refugees like Moshe to think 'only of the future', the only future for the Jews lies in their physical transference to a new geographical homeland (NB 11–12).

At this point in the novel, Stephan's reflections about the Jewish liberation from Nazi Germany are expanded towards another liberation, this time, that of 21-year-old Eva, who awaits

her imminent liberation from one of the Nazi concentration
camps at the end of the war. Her 'liberation', however, is as
ambiguous and uncertain as Moshe's expectation of Jewish
resettlement to the promised land of Israel:

> I watch as the trucks come roaring into the camp, dust and mud
> flying behind their wheels. The men jump down . . . and shout to
> each other. Then silence descends over them. They shield their eyes
> and look about themselves in disbelief. Silence. . . . This silent scene
> of us facing them. Skeletons facing men. Former prisoners facing
> liberators. We will no longer have to endure this captivity. We are
> free. Some among us begin to stumble and crawl towards the men.
> Weeping. Bodies twisting in bony gestures of supplication. . . . I have
> no strength to be happy. (NB 12–13)

Although Eva understands that the soldiers' arrival 'today, and
not some later day', means that she will survive the denigrating
ordeal of the camp, others around her 'continue to die in their
own excrement', their bodies, like her own, covered in lice, their
bodies 'withered', heads 'stubbled', their teeth 'broken or
misdirected'. Those who have 'survived' the camp have become
depersonalized, homogenized, 'grotesque figures . . . monkey-
people with shaved heads' who merely glance around and
'whisper warnings' (NB 165, 169). Eva, like Stephan, has survived
the Holocaust, but, while he endeavours to concentrate his
thoughts on the future, her present is suffocated by the traumas
of the past. Like many others in the camp, she has 'forgotten
how to think of tomorrow', her mind continually occupied by
her last conversation with her mother and her sister, Margot: 'I
roll on to my side and steer my thoughts towards Margot. She is
all I have left. If I can find Margot, then perhaps together we
might rebuild a life' (NB 17). Like Othello, Eva understands that
her sense of disorientation and abandonment is amplified by the
fact that there is 'nobody to guide [her] in the right direction'
(NB 24). Her only guide is her memory, an unreliable and
distorted entity that, together with her unconsciousness, further
increases her feelings of loneliness and despair: 'Margot! I sit on
her bed and watch as she picks up her suitcase . . . [She] pushes
me back . . . and starts to laugh. I still dream, one memory
swirling into another. Every night I endure an uncomfortable
journey to a place of distorted and unnecessary recollection . . .
Always the violence of memory' (NB 27, 33).

With the arrival of their liberators, the women in the camp, all except Eva, 'talk excitedly to each other' as they make plans for Palestine with a 'sudden and miraculous energy' (NB 45). Even though Eva does not participate in their enthusiastic planning, she listens to their 'talk' of diasporic wanderings with a silent fascination:

> Apparently, we have wandered long enough. We have worked and struggled too long on the lands of other peoples. The journey that we are making across the bones of Europe is a story that will be told in future years by many prophets. . . . I understand the passion that they must feel. I, too, have survived the storm. I, too, have dreamt of Palestine. (NB 45)

In order to enter into the present, Eva must break with the past – in other words, admit that there 'was never a Mama, neither in this camp nor in the last' and that there will 'never be a mama again' (NB 45–6). Instead, however, Eva's mind is full of questions that remain unanswered and unanswerable: 'Mama, why did we not all hide together? Mama, why did Papa not turn around and look at me?' (NB 47). Moreover, in a state of denial, Eva fails to accept her present condition, believing that she is 'different' from the other women in the camp, women whose faces have become 'ugly and ravaged . . . decaying now like discarded and foul-smelling fruit': 'I am not like them. I am not' (NB 48, 169). By creating a protective 'mask', Eva has been able to survive the horrors of the past, not only the mass genocide sweeping across Europe, but also her own experience of sexual assault.[20] With the words 'I am not like them', however, Eva too commits herself to a system of binaries dependent upon concepts of difference that have had a catastrophic effect upon world history. As she utters these words, the narrative switches abruptly from Eva's plight to another scene: that of fifteenth-century Venice, in the small town of Portobuffole, where the residents look forward to the return of the Venetian army, following the peace treaty with the 'infidel Turk' (NB 49).

Phillips situates this part of his narrative within Venice, not only because the city represented the centre of the Western Renaissance, and, by implication, Western culture and civilization, but because it also functioned as a powerful and extensive centre of colonial empire. The centre of 'culture' and 'civilization' is reconfigured in Phillips's text as an immense political and economic power, fuelled by cultural racism and colonization. Venice, as Phillips explains, was also the place in which the word 'ghetto' first originated. As described in the texts *Trent 1475* and *Portobuffole,* the term 'ghetto' was used to describe the section of Venice in which Jews were ordered to *live apart from* Christians following their expulsion in 1424 from Colonia, Germany, where they had been accused of occult beliefs and practices.[21] Thus, as Phillips's text examines the histories of peoples whose 'difference' has made them subjects of persecution and involuntary migration, the choice of Venice as the novel's location marks the onset of the diasporic condition and subsequent ghettoization in the modern world.

Regardless of the peace treaty between the Venetians and the Turks, the 'old suspicion of strangers' in seventeenth-century Venice remains predominant as the townsfolk seek out and hunt down anyone that they do not recognize. This distrust of others reaches a climax with the disappearance of the innocent beggar-child, Sebastian, whom the Christians believe has been sacrificed by the ghettoized Jews. Disturbed by their celebration of Passover, a feast designed to commemorate the Jews' escape from the Egyptian army as the Red Sea turned into 'blood', the Christians connect the 'disappearance' of Sebastian with suppositions about Jewish rituals involving blood such as anointment and circumcision, thereby reinforcing preconceptions about purity of blood and race (*NB* 51). As Phillips highlights the hysteria within the Christians' racialized responses, his novel also reveals the ways in which the Jews 'exploit' this level of conceived 'difference', as they distinguish themselves by wearing yellow stitching on their clothing and colonize the loan market. By exploiting the scriptural edict forbidding Christians to arrange loans amongst themselves, the Jews successfully argue that, because they are not technically 'brothers', they can give loans to Christians 'at whatever interest they deemed applicable' (*NB* 53).

> People detested the Jews for a variety of reasons, but the most often cited referred to their position in society as people who would loan money at interest, more often than not requiring extravagant security from the borrower. To comprehend fully how shameful a trade this was, one had to understand that Christians were strictly

forbidden to give out loans at interest to anyone. . . . Usury [thus became] a professional outlet for the Jews. The work was risky, and therefore profitable, but it was not physically demanding and it left time for both reading and studying. . . The [Jews'] money remained liquid, which further drove home the notion of the Jews maintaining a sybaritic lifestyle. (*NB* 53)

Barred from participating in any of the 'guilds' as either artists or tradesmen, the Jews turned to usury, which became the 'professional outlet' for them, a loophole that allowed the Republic of Venice to pretend that it was implementing a policy of tolerance, while obliging the Jews to lend money in exchange for permission to live in their territory (*NB* 53). Moreover, as Phillips's novel reveals, following the destabilization of the Venetian economy after the war with the Turks and the failure of expansionist projects in the Orient, the Venetian Grand Council realized that it could not afford to alienate the Jews if it was to benefit from large-scale capital investment for commercial and economic prospects inland. Thus, although the Jews' freedom was compromised by strict controls regarding their usury licence, their presence in Venice established a mode of capitalist venture that added momentum to colonial and transatlantic slave projects, enabling an economic and cultural 'rebirth' of the civilized Western world.

Throughout *Nature of Blood*, the importance of narrative in the creation or destruction of the self is clearly articulated. We are told that during the Passover the Jews *remember* the time during which they fled from Egypt, reciting the chants in which they configure themselves as slaves who will eventually become 'free' in the 'land of Israel': 'For three thousand years the Jews had . . . [recited] the same prayers, abstaining from the same foods . . . reading the same stories . . . This was the source of their safety . . . the basis of their relative confidence and happiness' (*NB* 58). Yet the status of narrative and 'truth' is also critiqued within Phillips's text, as the Venetian 'trial' against the Jews of Portobuffole in June 1480 is used to condemn the Jews for the murder of the young child Sebastian. Phillips takes for his literary source the documents relating to the trial of nineteen Jewish men and three Jewish women in 1475/6 for their alleged involvement in the ritual murder, in Trent, Italy, of a 2-year-old boy. The German manuscript of these trial proceedings, copied

65

around 1478, is known as the 'Yeshiva manuscript'. As R. Po Chia-Hsia suggests, the manuscript is 'a complex corpus, a compilation and translation of texts from different sources', incorporating the voices of Christian witnesses, Jews, magistrates, scribes and author-editors.[22] Consisting of over 600 folios of various testimonies, the 'Yeshiva manuscript' purports to tell the evil deeds of Jews in connection to the alleged ritual killing of Simon Unfer Dorben. These confessional statements were used to confirm and legitimize *post factum* previous Jewish executions and to 'expose' the barbarism of Jewish customs involving human blood. Despite the Latin inscription that validates the proceedings, 'Investigate scrupulously to find the truth with justice and clarity. Do not condemn anyone without a sincere and just trial', Phillips's text highlights the ways in which both the trial and the sentence are based upon gossip, murmurs and suppositions (*NB* 96).

But Phillips's text is not only concerned with the function of narrative and testimony in a historical sense. In the novel a clear comparison is made between the ghetto in which the Jews live in sixteenth-century Venice and Eva's hiding place within twentieth-century Europe. Like the legendary Anne Frank, Eva, a sexually and psychologically frustrated 16-year-old, has to 'remain hidden inside', able to stare only from a distance at a world that her parents have forbidden her from re-entering (*NB* 61). Ostracized and unstimulated, Eva finds herself staring at the atrocities that take place in front of her, like an involuntary witness of a spectacle from which she cannot sever herself: 'I felt ashamed. There was nothing normal about watching a boy dancing barefoot, one hand outstretched, his brother's corpse curled at his feet, and people slouching around them both as though neither of them were visible. Normal? I had almost forgotten the meaning of the word' (*NB* 64).

Historical sources dating back to the Holocaust have revealed that, like Eva, thousands of other Jews hid, concealed and confined themselves in spaces that became not only their prisons but their 'tombs'. Within these premature 'tombs', time and life became frozen, stretched amidst an eternal nightmarish dreamscape, as they lived literally 'petrified' of being betrayed 'by a gesture, a slip of a tongue or an accent': 'There was no midnight, there were no bells, there was no time' (*NB* 71).

Existing as if within an hypnotic trance, staring into mid-air so as to avoid the realities of the present, Eva tries to discover a reason for her people's persecution: 'People were hiding in every imaginable place. People were building tunnels under hallways, widening cellars, creating hiding places inside furniture, in woodlands, in fact everywhere. Until these ugly times passed by it was better to be safe. . . . How is it possible to be angry with people who have done you no wrong' (NB 92–3). While the Nazis engaged within a finely orchestrated programme of analysis, interpretation and (final) judgement, concealed victims scribbled, often in code, within the margins of holy books and diaries, as they tried to interpret the tragic events around them through the prism of their personal lives. Fragmented 'ghetto narratives' such as the Lodz Ghetto Chronicles and the Onez Shabbes reflected a collective effort to record and understand the brutal destruction of humanity while speaking 'with a strange confidence', as these 'authors' 'looked to history and literature for ways to respond to the Nazi onslaught'.[23]

Knowing in her heart that those who are hiding will eventually be discovered and killed, Eva fears that their very existence will be eradicated, not only from the historical records but also from the collective memory. Thus she understands the simultaneously fragile and tragic role of memory, as the only true preserve of historical events and individual lives: 'The newcomers [to the camp] must remember their names. Without a name, nobody will know who they are. . . . Only later will they appear in the Register of the Dead' (NB 169). Eva, however, like Othello, tries to sever her present self from that of her older, past self, in order to survive the traumas of the present: 'I try to forget my name. I decide to put Eva away in some place for safekeeping until all of this is over' (NB 165). Likewise, Othello's discovery of his 'blackness' and his developing racial consciousness coincides with the realization that he has also tried to escape, and thus, abandon his past:

[You] black uncle Tom . . . Fighting the white man's war for him . . . You tuck your black skin away beneath their epauletted uniform, appropriate their words, their manners, worry your nappy woollen head with anxiety about learning their ways, yet you conveniently forget your own family, and thrust your wife and son to the back of your mind. O strong man . . .O valiant soldier, O weak man. You are lost. (NB 181)

While Eva finds herself urgently speaking to Rosa as though her discovery of her sister, Margot, is an imminent certainty, she exposes her unrealistic belief in the reconciliation of her old life. Whilst her sense of urgency, together with her unshakeable belief in former securities, bears a strong resemblance to the urgency of the ghetto notes, her act of suicide highlights the perils, even the 'impossibilities', of cultural and post-traumatic crossings. Whereas Phillips's text presents us with a pessimistic version of cultural intermingling, it shies away from any insistence upon the stasis and isolation of cultures. Rather, Phillips suggests that, for cultural crossings to work without violence, those that 'cross' must find a way of connecting their past lives with their present, *without* the destruction of the self or of others.

The title of the novel, *The Nature of Blood*, highlights the correlation between racial and ancestral bloodlines within a fatally destructive social amphitheatre. The description of the death in seventeenth-century Venice of the three accused Jews, Moses, Giacobbe and Servadio, on the burning scaffold, where 'the blaze consumed flesh and blood', is mapped in turn onto the self-destruction of Othello, the 'black uncle Tom' who fights the white man's war, as well as the cremation chambers 'of a good red heat (approximately 800C)', to which Eva and other Jews, including her parents, travel in silence (*NB* 155–6). When the people on the death-train, whose faces take on a 'clenched weariness', see the fires burning in the distance, they search for clues that will help them to explain their present condition: 'The old, pregnant, young, short, infirm. This way, please . . . Where are we? . . . Where is God?' (*NB* 163).The persistent and unsettling question that permeates within Phillips's text – that is, 'what *is* the nature of blood?' – thus invokes its collorary, 'What is the nature of race?' *The Nature of Blood* suggests that there is no fixed, absolute answer to either of these questions. 'Race' is but a social category, a slippery signifier, while racialized discourse involves an 'arbitrary discursive operation'.[24] The nature of such a discursive regime is to separate, to divide and thereby to signify, through a process of displacement, a code of 'genetic' difference.

Whereas Fanon's work exposed the racially inflected system of power and representation, Phillips's text highlights the critical interconnection between the sufferings and injustices of people across time, from the fifteenth to the twentieth century. Through interweaving capitalist, commercial ideology with the practices of racial persecution, the future holds little promise of release from an established projectile of temporal repetition and persecution. In the same ways that Eva ashamedly associates her own survival with the death of others, the chronic anxiety, insomnia and shame of the survivors of the Holocaust are carried forward, without redemption from the memory of the past, into the future: 'I burn bodies. Burning bodies . . . Please do not let me discover anybody that I know' (*NB* 171–2). Indeed, once Eva has been liberated from the camp, her 'post-traumatic' state is neither 'post' nor past. She exists in a suspended state, a chronic state of 'emotional anaesthesia, or psychic numbing', detached from the present. Within such a nightmarish condition the possibility of purification is desperately ambiguous: 'Is this a dream? . . . How will they cleanse the world after this?' (*NB* 186).

In its examination of the causes and consequences of racism, *The Nature of Blood* succeeds in exposing the parallels between African and Jewish diasporic identity. According to David Theo Goldberg, Jewish identity consists of a historical consciousness that imagines a 'nomadic quest across [a] ceaseless duration of history'.[25] In this sense, blacks as well as Jews epitomize the peripatetic condition of postmodernity. Thus Uncle Stephen, whose words begin and end the narrative, speaks to the Holocaust survivors of their journey to the 'promised land'. Time for them does not follow a linear timescale but has become a nightmarish confusion of stultified pasts and futures. In a sense, both Stephen and Eva have entered their own 'black holes' in time, within a space that exists beyond the physical and in which the past is recalled in memory and compulsively repeated. Freud defined trauma as a significant rupture in memory, a lapse that in turn breaks continuity with the past. For this reason, in psychological terms, the traumatic event is repressed or denied. For the survivors of the Holocaust, survival meant a new form of imprisonment. On one level, survivors were often constrained to take on new identities and remain silent about the ways in which their old identities had been destroyed. On another level, the Holocaust survivor, although freed, entered into a 'new' condition of exile: although 'liberated' from the death-camp experience, these survivors continued to experience what they had 'died' through.

As Phillips's text points out and as Primo Levi has observed, for these survivors there was no triumph, only a groping for an adequate language to describe what they had been through. Their present, like Eva's, is saturated by a compulsion to 'look back':

> It has been observed by psychologists that the survivors of traumatic events are divided into two well-defined groups: those who repress their past *en bloc*, and those whose memory of the offence persists, as though carved in stone, prevailing over all precious or subsequent events. Now, not by choice but by nature, I belong to the second group. . . . I have not forgotten a single thing . . . memory continues to restore to me events, faces, words, sensations . . . not a detail was lost.[26]

In *The Nature of Blood*, both memory and language appear simultaneously *able and unable* to 'orchestrate past discords', able to gain strength through restatement and reaffirmation.[27] The overriding question, it seems, is not one about the 'nature of blood', but whether memory can offer any form, albeit fragile, of redemptive hope.

7

The Atlantic Sound

How long shall they kill our prophets?

(Bob Marley, 'Redemption Song')

As suggested by the chapter titles, 'Leaving Home', 'Homeward Bound', 'Home' and 'Exodus', Phillips's non-fictional work, *The Atlantic Sound* (2000), explores not only the complex notion of what constitutes ideas of home, but also the dislocations and discontinuities that have arisen from the historical 'prism' of the transatlantic slave trade. Phillips's text structures its exploration of home and exile within the modern condition of displacement and diaspora via a personal quest to three of the most important 'gateways' or cities of the triangular slave trade – Liverpool, Accra in Ghana and Charleston – as he repeats the 'rite of passage' he made as a child on his journey from the Caribbean to Britain during the 1950s. Despite the similar discomforts and quarrels he experiences as a voyager on this banana boat, Phillips, unlike his parents, is not a bewildered 'new' arrivant. For them, as for other post-war West Indian emigrants, such an Atlantic crossing was a journey into the unknown, a prelude to a larger adventure, which Phillips declares 'would change the nature of British history' (*AS* 4). For his parents, the long arduous journey across the Atlantic to Britain after the Second World war was a journey mitigated by a belief in the 'mother country's' desire to welcome and protect the children of its empire, an optimism that was quickly abandoned as West Indian emigrants found that Britain had little desire to 'embrace' its colonial offspring. Displaying three flags of identification – the Liberian flag signifying its country of registration, the Costa Rican flag in order to acknowledge the 'ownership' of the waters in which it is sailing, and the bright yellow flag marked 'Del Monte Quality Bananan' to identify its trade – Phillips's journey on the cargo ship MV *Horncap* highlights the development in contemporary transatlantic global commercialism as the latter-day 'produce', the banana, is transported to Western super-markets by a crew made up of refugees from Burma.

In the chapter entitled 'Leaving Home', Phillips visits Liverpool, one of the most important European cities of the eighteenth-century transatlantic slave trade. Citing words from Richard Wright's *Black Power* (1954), Phillips identifies the cultural amnesia which he believes has suppressed the city's sense of historical consciousness for over two centuries: 'How calm, innocent, how staid Liverpool looked in the June sunshine! What massive and solidly built buildings! . . . Along the sidewalks men and women moved unhurriedly. Did they ever think of their city's history?' (*AS* 74). Despite its former grandeur, Liverpool appears to Phillips as a city in a crumbling state of decline and irrational urban planning, a place where the past casts a 'deep shadow', the present 'grubby and inadequate'. It is a disquieting place, a city in which history is 'so physically present, yet so glaringly absent from people's consciousness' (*AS* 93). Phillips's visit to Liverpool prompts him to contemplate what he considers the 'modern condition' of Liverpool's citizens – that is, the 'cynical wit and a clinical depression' that he believes has arisen from the repressed memory of the past and that he associates with the dark 'shadowy' figure of 'Heathcliff', a 7-year-old child 'as dark as if it came from the devil' who haunts Emily Brontë's popular novel, *Wuthering Heights* (*AS* 92).

The second 'Liverpool-based' historical character that Phillips's text 'revisits' is not a fictional depiction, but that of John Emmanuel Ocansey who boarded the British ship SS *Mayumba* in April 1881 and arrived in Liverpool a few months later. As Phillips narrates in *The Atlantic Sound*, Ocansey had travelled from the British territory known as the Gold Coast to Liverpool in order to discover the fate of an extremely large amount of money (£2,678) accrued from the sale of African goods dispatched by his father, William Narh Ocansey, to a Liverpudlian commission agent called Robert Hickson. Hickson had taken the goods (mainly palm oil) from Ocansey's father in Africa on the understanding that he would sell them in Liverpool and use the profits to buy a steam-powered river launch or 'smoking canoe' on his behalf and thus increase the rate of transfer of goods from the African interior to the West. As detailed in his journal, Ocansey's experience upon the SS *Mayumba* was an extremely lonely one, and his arrival in Liverpool, a city's whose wealth in the eighteenth and nineteenth centuries had originated almost exclusively from the trade in slaves, was equally as alienating and depressing as he travelled amongst Liverpool's 'maze of wet and dry docks'.

Ships sailing from Liverpool to West Africa and then the Americas transported an average of 28,000 slaves per year. Hence, between 1783 and 1793, Liverpudlian ships transported goods from Britain to West Africa, where they were exchanged for in excess of 300,000 Africans. These 'slaves' were then transported to the Americas, where they were sold at a value of £15 million, thus enriching Liverpool merchants with a profit that was 'simply enormous'. Fifteen years prior to Ocansey's arrival in Liverpool, slavery had been abolished in all British territories. However, the 'shadow' of the trade still remained, as Liverpool became a 'gateway' for exploitative trade with China and the chief port for thousands of poverty-stricken Europeans intent upon migration to Australia and America during the late nineteenth and early twentieth centuries.

Soon after arriving in Liverpool, Ocansey learned that his father's agent had been declared bankrupt and that he, like many others, had been cheated by the British trading company. He found himself at the mercy of the English legal system, his case eventually being heard before Mr Justice Lopes in Liverpool's Crown Court in July 1881. Although Hickson was sentenced to fifteen months' imprisonment 'with hard labour', having been found guilty of obtaining money by false pretences, Ocansey received no more than two shillings and sixpence compensation and thus returned to Africa having recovered neither his father's money nor his travel expenses. Phillips's engagement with the Ocansey trial serves not only to remind his readers of the injustices suffered by slaves and African traders alike, but to critique the ideological concepts of democracy and 'civilization' at the heart of Western philosophy and European culture. Thus, the Ocansey episode as it is narrated in *The Atlantic Sound* exposes the 'blood money' at the heart of Western 'civilization', together with the injustices of a 'democratic' legal system that fails both its native and its colonial citizens. As Phillips uncovers a 'hidden history' within Liverpool, the grandeur of the city's buildings are revealed as testaments to the immoral and exploitative trade of Africans and other 'exotic' goods. In the second chapter, entitled 'Homeward Bound', Phillips heads for West Africa. On board a plane bound for Accra, he is troubled by the innocently repeated question, 'Where are you from?':

> And now . . . the same clumsy question. Does he mean, who am I? Does he mean, do I belong? Why does this man not understand the complexity of his question? I make the familiar flustered attempt to answer *the* question. He listens, and then spoils it all. 'So, my friend, you are going home to Africa. To Ghana.' I say nothing. *No, I am not going home.* (*AS* 98)

Phillips's frustration with the assumed 'simplicity' of concepts of 'home' and 'belonging' is reflected by the chapter headings 'Exodus' and 'Homeward Bound', which, taken in sequence, trouble conventional definitions of geographical and cultural orientation. While he sees himself as quite different from his African acquaintances, and indeed envies their sense of cultural stability – 'unlike me, he is an African . . . A whole man, a man of one place' – when Phillips arrives at the airport, the 'final gatekeeper' of the customs hall welcomes him in a language he does not understand. After what he ironically describes as a 'triple rite of passage' – obligatory health check, immigration and customs procedure – Phillips is met by Mansour, a young Ghanaian who has agreed to work with him as a guide. However, having arrived at the 'homeland', Phillips finds that Mansour, like many other Africans, is eager to leave Africa, having once already been deported from Britain as an illegal immigrant. Indeed, Phillips finds Mansour's dreams of escaping to a life 'outside Ghana' as disturbing and disappointing as the country's ex-minister of culture, Ben Abdullah's wish to 'escape' to America.

This endless repetition of migration and dispossession amidst various points of the original triangular trade proves to be a sticking point in Phillips's analysis of 'home'. Although he tries not to condemn or judge Mansour's aspirations, he is still critical of his motives: 'Here before me was a man who had served time in a British prison for being an illegal immigrant, asking me to help him to become an illegal immigrant in the United States . . . the overwhelming fact [was] that he had returned with nothing' (*AS* 110). Part of Phillips's disgruntlement stems from his definition of 'home' as a place in which members of the black diaspora could be 'free from the stigma of race'. Whilst the founding of settlement-countries such as Sierra Leone and Liberia offered 'homes' to which the former British and American slaves could return, the aspirations and expectations of many of these returnees clashed with the traditions of those that had remained within the 'homeland'. In repeating some of the critiques of Pan-African reunification articulated by activists and thinkers such as Frederick Douglass, Phillips finds himself out of tune with the ideas of 'return' popularized by more contemporary activists such as Marcus Garvey. According to Dr Abdullah, pan-Africanism involves the 'solidarity and cohesion of all Africans and peoples of African descent', a solidarity that he explains can be achieved via a resuscitation of African values prior to both the intrusion of Europe and what he terms the 'production' of 'Eurocentric Africans'. However, Phillips's re-telling of Ocansey's plight in the eighteenth century has already highlighted the fact that contact between Africans and Europeans was encouraged and maintained by both parties; in fact, Phillips's exploration of the African 'past' suggests that economic and financial values were already part of African culture *prior* to its contact with Europe. As Phillips resists what he views as a nostalgic and 'imaginative' return to the past, Dr Abdullah explains that the rescue of past values does not necessarily involve a 'going back', but a 'moving forward', a comment that serves further to highlight the plight of 'developing' countries such as Ghana:

> Europe has grafted her ways on to ours . . . 'Our' best way forward is to look to the past and see what we left back there, and then make sure that there is nothing there that we should have brought with us to the present . . . We still think of a Westminster model or a Washington model as democracy. That is not democracy, that is Western democracy. But before Western democracy there was African democracy, but I believe we have forgotten that somewhere in the past. (*AS* 115–16)

Dr Abdullah's aspirations to preserve some of the values of Africa's pre-colonial political systems, medicines, languages and methods of conservation and thereby to reinstate its 'natural evolution' contain some logic, but Phillips's text exposes some of the important idiosyncrasies and weakness within his argument. For Abdullah, slavery was not a 'European crime' by which Africans were captured and subjugated to a system of slave labour and plantocracy, but a 'punishment' for 'bad Africans' who in some respects 'got what they deserved'; likewise he believes that the slave fort at Cape Castle functioned as a 'school' for African children. Moreover, Abdullah's trace of world history envisages not a sequence of clashes and contact between cultures, but one in which cultures would under normal circumstances evolve 'naturally' and without interruption, while his account of the cessation of older African values fails to consider the ways in which such values and beliefs have *survived* the 'middle passage' and, indeed, continued to evolve within the diaspora.

Phillips's travels take him to an African-American called Dr Robert Lee, who was born in South Carolina, grew up in Charleston, studied in New York and eventually 'emigrated' to Ghana in the 1950s. Lee's analyses of European racism and the continued – albeit more sophisticated – 'plantation system' in the USA are far more in tune with Phillips's own critique of the unbalanced socio-economic and psychological conditions predominant within the modern world, and the function of tourism and global commercialism as a new form of the same old 'transatlantic' trade. According to Lee, Africans (within Africa) exist 'within a net of [historical] misinformation':

> These forts are the places where Africans were separated and the African sense of self was broken. . . . [But] the African doesn't really understand the slave trade. . . . To bring it up causes him embarrassment. If they can make money out of turning these places into shrines of tourism for Africans in the diaspora to come back and weep and wail and gnash their teeth, then so be it. They're businessmen. But to go deeper into the psychological and historical import of the slave trade is not what most Africans wish to do. (*AS* 121)

The tangle of diasporan loyalty and complexity appears to thicken, however, as Lee derides the group of African-Americans who, disappointed in the USA, have 'returned' to

Elmina in order to be 'Africans' again. Elmina, derived from the Portuguese term 'A Mina', the mine, functioned as early as 1471 as the commercial gateway between Europe and Africa on account of the abundance of gold mines that lay in its vicinity. Fascinated by the golden ornaments decorating the bodies of local Africans, Europeans began to trade in Africa with great vigour, culminating in the completion of the great 'castle' at Elmina by 600 Portuguese stonemasons, carpenters and workmen. With the completion of this European 'post' within Africa, commercial contact with the hinterland could be maintained within a mosquito-free environment. However, while Elmina originally functioned as a 'large, multi-ethnic, multi-lingual centre' of trade, by the middle of the sixteenth century, as *The Atlantic Sound* reveals, the most profitable cargo had become not gold, but human cargo.

For this reason, the historical site at Elmina appears to offer its potential both as a logical site for pan-African celebrations, *and* as a Holocaust memorial site to those Africans killed or dispossessed during the slave trade. Corrupted by the bureaucracy of the Ghanaian government, however, the status of Elmina remains ambiguous, and the Panafest 'celebration' of the arts, creativity and intellectual achievements of the Pan-African world that Phillips attends is embarrassingly badly organized and poorly attended. The opening performance, spoken in Fante with no translation, starts an hour and a half late, and is attended by an audience decorated with an assortment of trophies of Western capitalism, such as Nike trainers, without any consciousness of the commercial exploitation or global markets to which they testify. As the Panafest 'celebration' becomes a national embarrassment, with intoxicated youths gyrating to hi-life music and waving the Ghanaian flag, the 'animal-loving cousins' of the diaspora protest about the pending sacrifice of a ram for all 'those ancestors who shed their blood for the cause of slavery' (*AS* 137). Whilst the 'Day of Memorial and Remembrance' recognizes only males in the diaspora – Malcolm X, Steve Biko, Marcus Garvey, Patrice Lamumba and Martin Luther King – the tragicomedy continues as the Caribbean pilgrims to the Pan-Fest, who refer to their hosts as 'you Africans', have to be expelled from their hotel for ingesting 'certain substances' (*AS* 138). Cringing at the master of ceremonies' order to embrace other members of the audience and declare their love for one another, Phillips quits 'Panafesting' prematurely, having decided that not only is this 'family reunion' not working, but, given the diverging ideological differences across the diaspora and the little faith that Africans such as Mansour have in their homeland, it cannot work: 'The only way up in Ghana is out . . . That is how you progress in Ghana. You leave' (*AS* 157).

In 1919, Du Bois declared that 'the African movement means to us what the Zionist movement must mean to the Jews, the centralization of the race effort and the recognition of a racial front'.[1] In *Atlantic Sound* Phillips not only exposes the 'international face of racism' against which belief in diasporan unity is pitched, but also critiques enticing models of 'return' in which the inheritance of Africa may be seen to be carried backwards through time: 'I remember the words that a Zimbabwean writer once shared with me; the sea, he said, carries Africa on her back like an island' (*AS* 160).

Whereas Garvey and his followers had promoted a biblical vision involving the 'release' of blacks from their 'bondage' in America, this was interpreted quite literally as a desired exodus from the USA back to Africa, 'the promised land, the land of the ancestors'. In particular, some 'followers' reinforced the similarities between the African and the Zionist movements, by taking up the Hebrew traditions and lifestyles that they believed had been practised before the onset of the Atlantic slave trade. Inspired by the preachings of Rabbi Josiah Ford, who led a group of African-Americans to Ethiopia in 1930, these Hebrew Israelites formed congregations in Liberia, in the Ivory Coast and even in the Negev Desert in Israel. To Phillips's disappointment, however, these returnees believe that the 'diaspora' constitutes a 'diseased condition' from which they can be 'cleansed' upon their return to Africa. Moreover, Phillips's text criticizes these 'pilgrims' for chastising the USA as a place of the past and expecting Africa to solve their psychological problems and heal their wounds in order that they may return to 'Babylon' cleansed and sinless: 'If Africa fails them . . . [or] disappoints . . . they accuse "these" Africans of catering to the white men. Do they not understand. Africa cannot cure. Africa cannot make anybody feel whole. Africa is not a psychiatrist' (*AS* 173).

Envisaging itself as an 'amalgam' of persistence, vision and adaptability', this community of black Hebrews shuns profanity, homosexuality and 'obscene music', and idealizes the land of Israel as the spiritual centre of the world. It is, as Phillips ironically comments, an image of a disease-free world 'packaged and presented as though it were a celestial compound of heaven here on earth' (*AS* 171). For Phillips, one of the 'lessons' of the diaspora, and especially the concept of 'pilgrimage' to Africa, can be learned from the experiences of Phillips Quaque, an African missionary sponsored by the SPG who was stationed as a chaplain in the African slave fort at Cape Coast Castle for fifty years during the eighteenth century. Quaque had 'returned' to his own people in 1766 having married an Englishwoman named Catherine Blunt. His ensuing bitterness and disappointment, following the early death of his wife, the failure of his school at Cape Coast and the deep conflict between his own 'religiously inspired ambitions' and the military interests of the Company of Merchants who paid him to serve as chaplain, highlight the complexities of assimilation and the impossibilities of return to a homeland that, unlike its imaginary corollary, is not impervious to the forces of change or ruthless commercialism. As Phillips indicates, in many ways, Quaque, on return to Africa, is as alone as he was in England; for him the native Africans are uncivilized, ignorant of the Christian message and educational values that he has come to preach.

In the final chapter, entitled 'Home', Phillips visits Charleston, originally 'Charles Town', in South Carolina, the third important 'gateway' of the Atlantic slave trade where over 30 per cent of the African population first landed in the North American world. Having crossed the middle passage and been 'seasoned' and 'quarantined' in enormous pens known as 'pest houses', approximately 10,000 African slaves entered the port of Charles Town each year (*AS* 186). Consequently, by 1783, Charleston could enjoy its status as the most important port between Philadelphia and the Caribbean. What fascinates Phillips is the fact that this city, located at the centre of a vast network of transatlantic commerce founded upon slave labour, also produced Judge Waring, the son of a well-respected and established family whose own 'founding father' had migrated and settled in South Carolina in 1683. Having studied law, not at law school but at night, Julius Waties Waring passed the bar exam in 1902 and for most of his employment as City Attorney for Charleston maintained the racial prejudices of his birth and status. However, soon after his divorce from his first wife and his marriage to Elizabeth Avery in 1945, Judge Waring's condemnation of racist prejudice in the south and his subsequent Civil Rights decisions marked him as a judge with a 'passion for justice' (*AS* 197). Phillips's interviews with the friends and opponents of Judge Waring reveal him to have been considered both a traitor for disrupting what was considered the 'natural order' of life in the American South during the late 1940s and a champion for blacks on account of his condemnation of the systems of white supremacy and slaveocracy, which he believed contravened the tenets of freedom and democracy advocated by the American Constitution. Moreover, in addition to these radical demands, Waring overturned many of the discriminatory practices within the legal system itself, most especially its exclusion of blacks from the elective process, declaring in 1947 that it was 'time for South Carolina to rejoin the Union' (*AS* 198). By 1948, Waring's recommendations, together with support from both the NAACP and the Supreme Court, had enabled 35,000 blacks to vote in the state primaries, but as a consequence Waring and his wife found themselves branded 'monsters' and 'nigger-lovers' and ostracized from the social circles of their 'hometown' (*AS* 198).

In January 1950, Waring's wife, Elizabeth Waring, spoke openly and passionately about the injustices of race relations within the USA, praising blacks for their 'spiritual' stoicism and depicting white southerners as 'a sick, confused and decadent people . . . full of pride and complacency' (*AS* 111). Judge Waring continued to accuse the southern states of having a 'white' rather than a 'negro problem' and Elizabeth Waring spoke in favour of interracial marriage on NBC's televised programme, *Meet the Press* (*AS* 201). While the case known as *Briggs* v. *Elliot* failed to overturn the legitimacy of the South's 'separate but equal' policy, Waring's written opinion of the trial[2] became a landmark document in the struggle for civil rights and influenced the famous *Brown* v. *Board of Education* case heard two years later, which eventually brought an end to legalized segregation in the USA: 'Segregation in education can never produce equality and . . . it is an evil that must be eradicated. . . . I am of the opinion that all of the legal guideposts, expert testimony, common sense and reason point unerringly to the conclusion that the system of segregation in education . . . must go and must go now. *Segregation is* per se *inequality'* (*AS* 206). In his account of Waring, Phillips demonstrates his admiration for the Judge and his wife's determination to fight for the dignity and equality of all people regardless of colour. His exposure of their experiences of social ostracism highlights the penalties of such bravery, as they became 'banished from the hearts to which [they had once] turned', and 'exiled' from their own home and 'forced' to leave for New York (*AS* 203).

Phillips's epilogue to *Atlantic Sound* takes its readers to the 'dust of the desert', the settlement of African-Americans who have left the 'land of great captivity' and established themselves as the 'true children of Israel' in the small desert town of Dimona. Although Phillips uses the words of Martin Luther King to describe this community as being 'free at last', his tone is deeply ironic; their 'home' is little more than a settlement in which families live crowded together in small houses. It is, as he describes, 'a desert region', a 'military zone' over which jets fly threateningly: 'They tell me they have come home. To a world that does not recognize them. To a land they cannot tame' (*AS* 216). For Phillips, these black American 'Hebrews' are as ghettoized and self-segregated as the Jews described within his earlier work, *The Nature of Blood*. Within their constructed schema of redemption, their 'return' to their 'home' in Israel, the Holy Land in North Africa, makes manifest their 'freedom' from the 'great captivity' that was slavery. The pathos with which Phillips describes this 'utopia-in-the-desert' is made paramount within his text; as a 'closed society', this 'utopia' unwillingly continues the 'great captivity' from which it believes it has escaped, believing itself to be 'untouched' by the economic and political dramas that take place upon its periphery. Moreover, believing itself to be cleansed of 'social' diseases such as homosexuality, aids and cancer, such a society not only continues the social stigmas of 'difference' that have fuelled the fires of racial prejudice and religious fundamentalism, but makes itself vulnerable to the exposure of the 'lie' that is being lived. While these people believe that they are the 'chosen ones' who have returned from America and Africa to the promised land of Israel, Phillips emphasizes the reality of their 'stateless' condition and what he considers their misguided interpretations of biblical traditions. For this reason, the question posed by their Minister of Information – 'Do you not understand?' – remains both unanswered *and* unanswerable. Amidst this group of black Israelites Phillips is as isolated and distanced as Waring must have felt in his own home town. As an 'unbeliever', as someone who challenges the biblical model upon which these Hebrew Israelites have grafted their atemporal sense of history, Phillips's appears not to belong within this great diasporan family.

Indeed, for Phillips, there can be no meaningful severance of the past from the present. The plight of these 'black Hebrew Israelites' is as much an echo, or a continuation, of the sufferings and dispossession felt by their ancestors, and will remain so until 'home' is revisioned within a psychological, rather than territorial or geographical schema. For him, the 'past surges like a mighty river'; in other words, the endeavour to move backwards against the current towards the past, towards some imaginary point of 'origin' or 'home', is pointless (*AS* 220). As demonstrated by the structural framework of *The Atlantic Sound*, within Phillips's analysis the past is not 'left behind', but instead 'flows into' the present, thereby creating the possibility of new transformation. Thus, while the Hebrew Israelites try to hide their 'cultural baggage' by severing their connection from the present state of world affairs and returning to a *fictionalized* ancient past, the 'pop' songs[3] sung by their children advocate a vision of cultural intermixture that they cannot prevent: 'There is no closure. There will be no closure. . . . This landscape . . . says [the minister]. It is beautiful. . . . I say nothing. There is nothing I can say . . . Exodus. It is futile to walk into the face of history. As futile as trying to keep the dust from one's eyes in the desert' (*AS* 220–1).

8

Conclusion

In a speech delivered in Nashville, Tennessee, on 27 December 1962, the orator, civil-rights leader and essayist Martin Luther King presented an eloquent defence of his philosophy of racial integration, as distinct from the legal and social processes of desegregation:

> The problem of race and color prejudice remains America's greatest moral dilemma. When one considers the impact it has upon our nation, internally and externally, its resolution might well determine our destiny. History has thrust upon our generation an indescribably important task – to complete a process of democratization which our nation has too long developed too slowly, but which is our most powerful weapon for world respect and emulation. How we deal with this crucial situation will determine our moral health as individuals, our cultural health as a region, our political health as a nation, and our prestige as a leader of the free world. The shape of the world today does not afford us the luxury of an anemic democracy. The price that America must pay for the continued oppression of the Negro is the price of its own destruction. The hour is late; the clock of destiny is ticking out; we must act now before it is too late.[1]

For King, therefore, time, or the clock of destiny, was to be measured against the urgent need to establish integration amongst blacks and whites, a condition necessary to what he perceived as 'a recognition of the fact that a denial of freedom to an individual is a denial of life itself': 'I may do well in a *desegregated* society but I can never know what my total capacity is until I live in an *integrated* society. I cannot be free until I have had the opportunity to fulfil my total capacity untrammeled [*sic*] by any artificial hindrance or barrier.'[2] King's demand for racial integration strategically acknowledged both the 'solidarity of the human family' and the pursuit of freedom as a fundamental prerequisite for choice, determination and responsibility. King defined the Civil Rights March on Washington in August 1963 as the 'greatest demonstration *for freedom* in the history of our nation'.[3] In his famous 'I Have a Dream' speech, he defined the 'Negro' as an 'exile in his own land', crippled by the manacles of segregation, discrimination and materialism. According to King, 1963 was not 'an end, but a beginning', a 'dream' witnessing the possible transformation of the nation 'into an oasis of freedom and justice': 'This is our hope. This is the faith that I go back to the South with . . . "Free at last, free at last, thank God Almighty, we are free at last." '[4]

In a wide-ranging collection of fictional and non-fictional work, Caryl Phillips responds to the posthumous description of King as 'the conscience of his generation' ('His life informed us, his dreams sustain us'), addressing and transforming his predecessor's visions of individual freedom and racial integration.[5] In Phillips's work, however, King's ticking 'clock of destiny' is translated into a concept of time in which the dimensions of the collective experience of the black diaspora are prioritized. Occupying both coordinates of space and time, Phillips's representation of the black diaspora emphasizes not only the correlation between past, present and future, but the simultaneous processes of loss and recovery necessary for visionary transformation. In Phillips's work, therefore, memory, and thus recovery of past events, is a fragile yet fundamental process by which a sense of continuity and radical agency can be maintained amidst a historical 'landscape' of cultural trauma, suffering and loss. Phillips's engagement with concepts of time and space, or what I have referred to as the 'black hole schema', reminds us that without memory, without reading the traces of the past, the recognition and tolerance of difference, albeit individual, cultural, or political, are severely jeopardized.[6] Moreover, Phillips's schema reminds us that the processes of cultural memory challenge indoctrinated concepts of time and highlight the temporal status of memory as an aspect not of the past, but of the present.[7]

> Memory, like love, gains strength through restatement, reaffirmation; in a culture through ritual, tradition, stories, art. Memory courts our better selves; it helps us recognize the importance of deed; we learn from pleasure just as we learn from pain. And when memory evokes consideration of what might have been or been prevented, memory becomes redemptive . . . 'To remember is a kind of hope.'[8]

Notes

CHAPTER 1. TIME AND THE BLACK DIASPORA

1. William Fordyce Mavor, *History of the Dispersion of the Jews; of Modern Egypt; and of other African Nations* (London, 1802). This volume formed part of Mavor's multi-volume work, *Universal History: Ancient and Modern, from the Earliest Records of Time, to the General Peace of 1801*, 25 vols. (London, 1802–4). See also Bryan Edwards, *The History, Civil and Commercial, of the West Indies* (Dublin, 1793), vol. ii.
2. Edward Wilmot Blyden, *Christianity, Islam and the Negro Race* (London: W. B. Whittingham and Co., 1887); ed. Christopher Fyfe (Edinburgh: Edinburgh University Press, 1967), 120. See also James Africanus Beale Horton, *Letters on the Political Condition of the Gold Coast* (London, 1870).
3. W. E. B. Du Bois, *Dusk of Dawn: An Essay toward an Autobiography of a Race Concept* (New York: Harcourt, Brace and Co., 1940); repr. in *W. E. B. Du Bois: The Oxford Reader*, ed. Eric Sundquist (New York: Oxford University Press, 1996), 95. See also Sir Harry Johnston, *The Negro in the New World* (London: Methuen, 1910).
4. Paul Gilroy, *The Black Atlantic: Modernity and Double Consciousness* (London: Verso, 1993), 111. See also Martin Kitson and Robert Rotberg, *The African Diaspora: Interpretive Essays* (Cambridge, Mass., Harvard University Press, 1976).
5. Bruce King, *West Indian Literature* (London: Macmillan, 1995), 11.
6. Rosalind Bell, 'Worlds Within: An Interview with Caryl Phillips, *Callaloo*, 14/3 (1991), 578–606.
7. Renu Juneja, *Caribbean Transactions: West Indian Culture in Literature* (London: Macmillan, 1996), 7.
8. John Samuel Mbiti, *African Religions and Philosophy* (1969; repr. London: Heinemann, 1990), 15–25.
9. St. Augustine, *Confessions*, ed. Maria Boulding (London: Hodder & Stoughton, 1997), 11: 14, 295–6.
10. Plato, *The Dialogues of Plato*, ed. B. Jowett, 4 vols. (Oxford: Clarendon Press, 1953).

11. Peter Osbourne, *The Politics of Time: Modernity and Avant Garde* (London: Verso: 1995), p. viii; Paul Davies, *About Time: Einstein's Unfinished Revolution* (Harmondsworth: Penguin, 1995), 23. Einstein, like Phillips, was also concerned with the establishment of Palestine as a homeland for the diasporic Jews.

12. Isaac Newton, *The Principia: Mathematical Principles of Natural Philosophy* (1687), trans. Bernard Cohen and Anne Whitman (Berkeley and Los Angeles: University of California Press, 1999), frontispiece.

13. Ibid., frontispiece.

14. Ibid. See also Julian Barbour, *The End of Time: The Next Revolution in our Understanding of the Universe* (London: Weidenfeld & Nicolson, 1999).

15. Davies *About Time*, 22.

16. George Wilhelm Hegel, 'The Natural Context or the Geographical Basis of World History', *Lectures on the Philosophy of World History*, trans. H. B. Nisbet, ed. Duncan Forbes (Cambridge: Cambridge University Press, 1975), 190.

17. Ibid. 183–4.

18. Edmund Husserl, *Lectures on the Phenomenology of Internal Time-Consciousness*, trans. John Brough (Dordrecht: Kluwer, 1991), 3.

19. Osbourne, *The Politics of Time*, 11, 42. See also *The Fiery Brook: Selected Writings of L. Feuerback* (1972), 57–8.

20. Paul Ricoeur, *Time and Narrative*, trans. Kathleen McLaughlin and David Pellauer (Chicago: University of Chicago Press, 1988), vol. iii; Osbourne, *The Politics of Time*, 45.

21. Ricoeur, *Time and Narrative*, 127.

22. Ibid. 128.

23. Davies, *About Time*, 14.

24. Julian Barbour, *The End of Time: The Next Revolution in our Understanding of the Universe* (London: Weidenfeld & Nicolson, 1999), 12–13.

25. See Juneja's discussion of Gloria Naylor's *Praisesong for the Widow* in *Caribbean Transactions*, 50–64.

26. Hortense Spillers, in Spillers and Marjorie Pryse (eds.), *Conjuring Black Women: Black Women, Fiction and Literary Tradition* (Bloomington, Ind.: Indiana University Press, 1985), 166.

27. Stephen Hawking and Roger Penrose, *The Nature of Space and Time* (Princeton, NJ: Princeton University Press, 1996), 37.

28. Jonathan Franzen, 'The Long Slow Slide into the Abyss', *Guardian*, 15 December 2001, 15–21, 15.

29. Ibid. 17.

30. Walter Benjamin, 'Theses on the Philosophy of History' (1940), repr. in *Illuminations*, trans. Hannah Arendt (London: Fontana Press, 1992); Lois Parkinson Zamora, *The Usable Past: The Imagination of*

History in Recent Fictions of the Americas (Cambridge: Cambridge University Press, 1997) 156–7.

31. David Theo Goldberg, in Lemuel Johnson, *Shakespeare in Africa (and Other Venues). Import and the Appropriation of Culture* (Trenton, NJ: Africa World Press, 1998), 133.

32. Luis Bunuel, *Untimely Meditation*, cited in Andreas Huyssen, *Twilight Memories: Marking Time in a Culture of Amnesia* (London: Routledge, 1995).

33. Dominick La Capra, *History and Memory after Auschwitz* (Ithaca, NY: Cornell University Press, 1998).

34. Juneja, *Caribbean Transactions*, 50–64.

CHAPTER 2. *STRANGE FRUIT*

1. This production of Phillips's *Strange Fruit* was directed and designed by Jimo Rand and Louise Belson. Derek Walcott, *Henri Christophe: A Chronicle in Seven Sequences* (Bridgetown: Advocate Co., 1950). Errol John, *Moon on a Rainbow Shawl* (London: Faber & Faber, 1958).

2. Billie Holiday, 'Strange Fruit' (1939). The song 'Strange Fruit' was written by Abel Meeropol, who wrote under the name of Lewis Allen (1903–86).

3. Stuart Nicholson, *Billie Holiday* (London: Victor Gollancz, 1995), 113.

4. John White, *Billie Holiday: Her Life and Times* (London: Omnibus Press, 1988), 53–4; In 1944, Lillian Eugenia Smith, a white Southern and opponent of racial discrimination and segregation, published the US edition of her sensational novel *Strange Fruit [A Novel]* (London: Cresset Press, 1945), a tale of interracial love between a black man and a white woman.

5. James Procter (ed.), *Writing Black Britain, 1948–1998: An Interdisciplinary Anthology* (Manchester: Manchester University Press, 2000).

6. See Leopold Seghar Senghor, *The Africa Reader: Independent Africa* (London: Vintage, 1970), repr. in Patrick Williams and Laura Chrisman (eds.), *Colonial Discourse and Post-Colonial Theory: A Reader* (Hemel Hempstead: Harvester, 1994); W. E. B. Du Bois, *Dusk of Dawn: An Essay toward an Autobiography of a Race Concept* (New York: Harcourt, Brace and Co., 1940); repr. in *W. E. B. Du Bois: The Oxford Reader*, ed. Eric Sundquist (New York: Oxford University Press, 1996); Casely Hayford, *Ethiopia Unbound: Studies in Race Emancipation* (London: C. M. Phillips, 1911). Senghor described *negritude* as: 'Neither racialism nor self-negation. Yet it is not just affirmation; it is rooting oneself, and self-confirmation: confirmation of one's *being*. Negritude is nothing more or less than what some English-speaking Africans have called the *African personality*. It is no different from the

"black personality" discovered and proclaimed by the American Negro Movement. . . . Perhaps our only originality, since it was the West Indian poet Aimé Césaire who coined the word negritude, is to have attempted to define the concept a little more closely; to have developed it as a weapon, an instrument of liberation and as a contribution to the humanity of the twentieth century' (Senghor, in *Colonial Discourse*, 27).

7. Du Bois, *Dusk of Dawn*.
8. See Cyril Lionel Robert James, *History of Negro Revolt* (London, 1938; New York: Harkell Hone, 1969).
9. Frantz Fanon, *The Wretched of the Earth*, trans. Constance Farrington, ed. Jean-Paul Sartre (Harmondsworth: Penguin, 1990). According to Fanon in his chapter 'On National Culture, 'Colonialism . . . has never ceased to maintain that the Negro is a savage'.
10. Martin Luther King, *A Testament of Hope: The Essential Writings and Speeches of Martin Luther King, Jr.*, ed. James Washington (San Francisco: Harper Collins, 1991), 217, 220.
11. The Black Panthers, founded in 1966 in San Francisco by Huey Newton and Bobby Seale. In 1969, 27 members of the Black Panthers were killed by police and 749 arrested and jailed.
12. See Eugene Victor Wolfenstein, *The Victims of Democracy. Malcolm X and the Black Revolution* (Berkeley and Los Angeles: University of California Press, 1981).
13. Steven Lawson, *Running for Freedom: Civil Rights and Black Politics* (Philadelphia: Temple University Press, 1991), 126.
14. Ibid. 125.
15. Such a vision was shared by the radical organizations known as CORE and the SNCC, while Stokely Carmichael popularized the phrase 'black power'.
16. Malcolm X, *Autobiography of Malcolm X*, ed. Alex Hayley (London: Hutchinson, 1965), 256–7.
17. Aimé Césaire *Discourse on Colonialism*, trans. John Pinkham (London: Monthly Review Press, 1955).
18. See Robert Young, *Postcolonialism: An Historical Introduction* (Oxford: Blackwell, 2001), for a detailed discussion of the historical and theoretical analysis of the emergence and development of post-colonial theory and anti-colonial movements.
19. Henry Bretton, *The Rise and Fall of Kwame Nkrumah: A Study of Personal Rule in Africa* (London: Pall Mall, 1967), 16. See also Kwame Nkrumah, *Neo-Colonialism: The Last Stage of Imperialism* (London: Nelson, 1965); Young, *Postcolonialism*, 45.
20. John Hobson, *Imperialism: A Study* (1902; repr. London: George Allen & Unwin, 1938).
21. Young, *Postcolonialism*, 57.

22. Hence the title of Fanon's text, *Black Skin, White Masks* trans. Charles Lam Markmann (1952; repr. London: Pluto, 1986).
23. Richard Wright, *Native Son* (London: Victor Gollancz, 1940).

CHAPTER 3. *A STATE OF INDEPENDENCE*

1. Caryl Phillips, *Where There is Darkness* (Derbyshire: Amber Lane Press, 1982).
2. V. S. Naipaul, *Mimic Men* (London: Deutsch, 1967).
3. See Susheila Nasta (ed.), *Motherlands: Black Women's Writing from Africa, the Caribbean and South Asia* (London: Women's Press, 1991), for a full discussion of the relationship between mother empire and its colonies.
4. Frantz Fanon, *The Wretched of the Earth*, trans. Constance Farrington, ed. Jean-Paul Sartre (Harmondsworth: Penguin Books, 1990), 168.
5. Homi Bhabha, *The Location of Culture* (London: Routledge, 1994).

CHAPTER 4. *THE EUROPEAN TRIBE*

1. Karl Marx, *Political Writings*, vol. ii, trans. Ben Fowkes and Paul Jackson (Harmondsworth: Penguin, 1973); Robert Young, *Postcolonialism: An Historical Introduction* (Oxford: Blackwell, 2001) 278.
2. Rosalind Bell, 'Worlds Within: An Interview with Caryl Phillips', *Callaloo*, 14/3 (1991), 578–606, 589.
3. Claude McKay, *Banjo* (London: Harper and Bros., 1929).
4. Derek Walcott, *Midsummer* (London: Faber & Faber, 1984). See also Shakespeare's *The Tempest*.
5. See Ron Ramdin, *Reimaging Britain: Five Hundred Years of Black and Asian History* (London: Pluto, 1999), James Procter, *Writing Black Britain, 1948-1998: An Interdisciplinary Anthology* (Manchester: Manchester University Press, 2000), Houston Baker, Manthia Diawara and Ruth Lindeborg, *Black British Cultural Studies: A Reader* (Chicago: University of Chicago Press, 1996) and Paul Edwards and David Dabydeen, *Black Writers in Britain, 1760-1890* (Edinburgh: Edinburgh University Press, 1991).
6. Dick Hebdige, *Subculture: The Meaning of Style* (London: Routledge, 2002).
7. See M. Banton, *Race Relations* (London: Tavistock Publications, 1967); D. Hiro, *Black British, White British* (Harmondsworth: Penguin, 1972) and Colin MacInnes, *City of Spades* (London: Allison & Busby, 1957).
8. Stuart Hall, C. Critcher, T. Jefferson, J. Clarke and B. Roberts, *Policing the Crisis: Mugging, the State, and Law and Order* (London: Macmillan, 1978).

9. Ralph Ellison, *Invisible Man* (London: Victor Gollancz, 1953), Richard Wright, *Native Son* (London: Victor Gollancz, 1940) and Harold Cruse, *The Crisis of the Negro Intellectual* (London: W. H. Allen, 1969).

10. Ellison, *Invisible Man*, 1.

11. James Baldwin, *Evidence of Things Not Seen* (London: Joseph, 1986).

12. Aimé Césaire, *Discourse on Colonialism*, trans. John Pinkham (London: Monthly Review Press, 1955).

13. Karl Marx and Freidrich Engels, *Manifesto of the Communist Party* (Moscow: Progress Publishers, 1848; repr. 1952), 42–3.

CHAPTER 5. *CROSSING THE RIVER*

1. Fred D'Aguiar, 'Home is Always Elsewhere', in *Black British Culture and Society: A Text Reader*, ed. Kwesi Owusu (London: Routledge, 1999), 195–206, 201–2.

2. Edward Kamau Brathwaite, *History of the Voice: The Development of Nation Language in Anglophone Caribbean Poetry* (London: New Beacon, 1984), 55. See also his *The Development of Creole Society in Jamaica, 1770–1820* (Oxford: Clarendon Press, 1971).

3. Robert Fraser, *Masks: A Critical Review* (London: Collings, British Council, 1981) 17; Tony Ilona, *Wasafiri*, 2 (Autumn 1995), 3–9.

4. Edward Kamau Brathwaite, *The Arrivants: A New World Trilogy* (Oxford: Oxford University Press, 1967).

5. Phillip Quaque to the SPG, 17 January 1778; Thomas Peters and David Edmon, 23 December 1791; Susana Smith, 12 May 1792, Cato Perkins and Isaac Anderson, 25 October 1793; all cited in Paul Edwards and David Dabydeen, *Black Writers in Britain, 1760–1890* (Edinburgh University Press, 1991), 114, 85.

6. Two years earlier, another 'Cudjo' member, 'William', who had also travelled with Quaque under the auspices of the SPG, was 'put out of reach of instruction by a Lunacy' which seized him in December 1764 and led to his confinement in St Luke's Hospital and subsequent death in Guy's Hospital.

7. Edwards and Dabydeen, *Black Writers in Britain*, 101.

8. Edmund Blyden, *Christianity, Islam and the Negro Race* (1887), ed. Christopher Fyfe (Edinburgh: Edinburgh University Press, 1967).

9. Edmund Blyden, 'Sierra Leone: Origin, Work and Destiny' (April 1884), in *Christianity, Islam and the Negro Race*, 202.

10. Edmund Blyden, *The Problems before Liberia* (London: C. M. Phillips, 1909), 11–12, 20, 30.

11. See ibid. 1–2; Edward Wilmot Blyden, *The Aims and Methods of a Liberal Education for Africans: Inaugural Address* (Cambridge, Mass.: John Wilson, 1882), 17, 11.

12. Ilona, *Wasafiri*, 3-9. For example, texts by John Newton, Sir Francis Drake, Sir Richard Hawkyns and Richard Haklyt.
13. John Newton, *Letters to a Wife*, 2 vols. (London, 1793).
14. See Henry Louis Gates, *The Signifying Monkey: A Theory of Afro-American Literary Criticism* (Oxford: Oxford University Press, 1988).

CHAPTER 6. *THE NATURE OF BLOOD*

1. W. E. B. Du Bois, *The Souls of Black Folk* (New York: Bantam Books, 1903), 10.
2. Frantz Fanon, *Black Skin, White Masks*, trans. Charles Lam Markmann (1952; repr. London: Pluto, 1986).
3. Robert Young, *Postcolonialism: An Historical Introduction* (Oxford: Blackwells, 2001) 173-4.
4. Frantz Fanon, *The Wretched of the Earth*, trans. Constance Farrington, ed. Jean-Paul Sartre (1961; repr. Harmondsworth: Penguin, 1983), 106.
5. Anne Frank, *The Diary of Anne Frank* (London: Vallentine, Mitchell, Fine, 1953).
6. William Shakespeare, *Othello*, II. i. 293.
7. See Ben Okri, 'Meditation on Othello', *West Africa*, 30 March 1997, 610-19.
8. *Othello*, III. iii. 267-8.
9. *Othello*, I. iii. 260-4.
10. Fanon, *Black Skin, White Masks*, 84.
11. Zora Neale Hurston, 'How It Feels to be Colored Me' (1928); repr. in *The Norton Anthology of African-American Literature*, ed. Henry Louis Gates and Nellie Y. McKay (New York: Norton, 1997), 1009.
12. Frantz Fanon, *Toward the African Revolution* (Harmondsworth: Penguin, 1970), 63.
13. Fanon, *Black Skin, White Masks* 112, 109.
14. Lemuel Johnson, *Shakespeare in Africa (and Other Venues). Import and the Appropriation of Culture* (Trenton, NJ: Africa World Press, 1998), 133.
15. Hall, *The Fact of Blackness*, 19; Fanon, *Black Skin White Masks* 10.
16. Tony Ilona, *Wasafiri*, 2 (Autumn 1995), 3-9.
17. Paul Gilroy, *The Black Atlantic: Modernity and Double Consciousness* (London: Verso, 1993), 211-12.
18. Joel Beinen, *The Dispersion of Egyptian Jewry* (Berkeley and Los Angeles: University of California Press, 1998), 1.
19. See also Rushdie's and Kureishi's comments on 'imaginary homelands' in a post-colonial context.
20. See Fanon, *Black Skins, White Masks*.

21. R. Po-Chia Hsia, *Trent 1475: Stories of a Ritual Murder Trial* (New Haven, Conn.: Yale University Press, 1992).
22. Ibid., p. xxi.
23. Sara Horowitz, 'Voices for the Killing Ground', in *Voicing the Void: Muteness and Memory in Holocaust Fiction* (Albany, NY: University State of New York Press, 1997), 44. See also Liejan Dobroszycki, *The Chronicle for the Lodz Ghetto* (London: Yale University Press, 1984).
24. Hall, *The Fact of Blackness*, 21.
25. David Theo Goldberg and Michael Krausz, *Jewish Identity* (Philadelphia: Temple University Press, 1986), 30–1.
26. Primo Levi, Preface, *Moments of Reprieve*, trans. Ruth Feldman (London: Michael Joseph, 1986).
27. Lawrence Langer, 'Remembering Survival', 70; Anne Michaels, 'Cleopatra's Love', *Poetry Canada Review* (March 1994), 15.

CHAPTER 7. *THE ATLANTIC SOUND*

1. *W. E. B. Du Bois: The Oxford Reader*, ed. Eric Sundquist (New York: Oxford University Press, 1996), 639.
2. Judge Waties Waring, 23 June 1951, *Briggs v. Elliot*, District Court of the US for South Carolina Charleston Division, Civil Action no. 2657.
3. See Bob Marley, 'War' [quoting from Haile Selassie]: 'Until the philosophy which holds one race | Superior and another inferior | Is finally and permanently discredited and abandoned | Everywhere is war' (Harry Hawke, *The Complete Lyrics of Bob Marley. Songs of Freedom* (London: Omnibus, 2001)).

CONCLUSION

1. Martin Luther King, 'The Ethical Demands for Integration', in *A Testament of Hope: The Essential Writings and Speeches of Martin Luther King, Jr.* ed. James Washington (New York: Harper Collins, 1991), 117.
2. Ibid. 119, 121.
3. King, 'I Have a Dream', in ibid. 121, 217; emphasis added.
4. Ibid. 218, 219, 220.
5. Ibid. p. iv.
6. Andreas Huyssen, *Twilight Memories: Marking Time in a Culture of Amnesia* (London: Routledge, 1995), 252.
7. Ibid. 3.
8. Anne Michaels, 'Cleopatra's Love', *Poetry Canada Review* (March 1994), 15.

Select Bibliography

WORKS BY CARYL PHILLIPS

Novels

The Final Passage (London: Faber & Faber, 1985).
A State of Independence (London: Faber & Faber, 1986).
Higher Ground (London: Viking Press, 1989).
Cambridge (London: Bloomsbury Publishing, 1991).
Crossing the River (London: Bloomsbury Publishing, 1993).
The Nature of Blood (London: Faber & Faber, 1997).

Plays

Strange Fruit (Derbyshire: Amber Lane Press, 1981).
Where There is Darkness (Derbyshire: Amber Lane Press, 1982).
The Shelter (Oxford: Amber Lane, 1984).
The Wasted Years (London: Methuen, 1985).
Playing Away (London: Faber & Faber, 1987).
The Mystic Masseur (Trinidad: Paria Publishing Company, 2001).

Non-Fiction

The European Tribe (London: Faber & Faber, 1987).
Extravagant Strangers: A Literature of Belonging (London: Faber & Faber, 1997).
The Right Set: The Faber Book of Tennis (London: Faber & Faber, 1999).
The Atlantic Sound (London: Faber & Faber, 2000).
A New World Order: Selected Essays (London: Secker & Warburg, 2001).
A Distant Shore (London: Secker & Warburg, 2003).

SECONDARY READING

Baker, Houston, Diawara, Manthia, and Lindeborg, Ruth (eds.), *Black British Cultural Studies: A Reader* (Chicago: University of Chicago Press, 1996).

Baldwin, James, *Evidence of Things Not Seen* (London: Joseph, 1986).

Banton, M., *Race Relations* (London: Tavistock Publications, 1967).

Barbour, Julian, *The End of Time: The Next Revolution in our Understanding of the Universe* (London: Weidenfeld & Nicolson, 1999).

Beinen, Joel, *The Dispersion of Egyptian Jewry* (Berkeley and Los Angeles: University of California Press, 1998).

Bell, Rosalind, 'Worlds Within: An Interview with Caryl Phillips', *Callaloo*, 14/3 (1991), 578–606.

Benjamin, Walter, 'Theses on the Philosophy of History' (1940), repr. in *Illuminations*, trans. Hannah Arendt (London: Fontana Press, 1992).

Bhabha, Homi, *The Location of Culture* (London: Routledge, 1994).

Blyden, Edward Wilmot, *Liberia's Offerings* (London, 1862).

—— *The Aims and Methods of a Liberal Education for Africans: Inaugural Address* (Cambridge, Mass.: John Wilson, 1882).

—— *Christianity, Islam and the Negro Race* (1887), ed. Christopher Fyfe (Edinburgh: Edinburgh University Press, 1967).

—— *The Problems before Liberia* (London: C. M. Phillips, 1909).

Brathwaite, Edward Kamau, *The Arrivants: A New World Trilogy* (Oxford: Oxford University Press, 1967).

—— *The Development of Creole Society in Jamaica, 1770–1820* (Oxford: Clarendon Press, 1971).

—— *History of the Voice. The Development of Nation Language in Anglophone Caribbean Poetry* (London: New Beacon, 1984).

Bretton, Henry, *The Rise and Fall of Kwame Nkrumah: A Study of Personal Rule in Africa* (London: Pall Mall, 1967).

Césaire, Aimé, *Discourse on Colonialism*, trans. John Pinkham (London: Monthly Review Press, 1955).

Cruse, Harold, *The Crisis of the Negro Intellectual* (London: W. H. Allen, 1969).

D'Aguiar, Fred, 'Home is Always Elsewhere', in *Black British Culture and Society: A Text Reader*, ed. Kwesi Owusu (London: Routledge, 1999).

Davies, Paul, *About Time: Einstein's Unfinished Revolution* (Harmondsworth: Penguin, 1995).

Dobroszycki, Liejan, *The Chronicle for the Lodz Ghetto* (London: Yale University Press, 1984).

Du Bois, W. E. B., *The Souls of Black Folk* (New York: Bantam Books, 1903).

—— *Dusk of Dawn: An Essay toward an Autobiography of a Race Concept*

(New York: Harcourt, Brace and Co., 1940); repr. in *W. E. B. Du Bois: The Oxford Reader*, ed. Eric Sundquist (New York: Oxford University Press, 1996).

Edwards, Bryan, *The History, Civil and Commercial, of the West Indies*, 2 vols. (Dublin, 1793).

Edwards, Paul, and Dabydeen, David, *Black Writers in Britain, 1760–1890* (Edinburgh: Edinburgh University Press, 1991).

Ellison, Ralph, *Invisible Man* (London: Victor Gollancz, 1953).

Fanon, Frantz, *Black Skin, White Masks*, trans. Charles Lam Markmann (1952; repr. London: Pluto, 1986).

—— *The Wretched of the Earth*, trans. Constance Farrington, ed. Jean-Paul Sartre (1961; repr. Harmondsworth: Penguin, 1990).

—— *Toward the African Revolution* (Harmondsworth: Penguin, 1970).

Frank, Anne, *The Diary of Anne Frank* (London: Vallentine, Mitchell, Fine, 1953).

Franzen, Jonathan, 'The Long Slow Slide into the Abyss', *The Guardian* , 15 December 2001, 1521.

Fraser, Robert, *Masks: A Critical Review* (London: Collings, British Council, 1981).

Gates, Henry Louis, *The Signifying Monkey: A Theory of Afro-American Literary Criticism* (Oxford: Oxford University Press, 1988).

Gilroy, Paul, *The Black Atlantic: Modernity and Double Consciousness* (London: Verso, 1993).

Goldberg, David Theo, and Krausz, Michael, *Jewish Identity* (Philadelphia: Temple University Press, 1986).

Hall, Stuart, Critcher, C., Jefferson, T., Clarke, J., and Roberts, B., *Policing the Crisis: Mugging, the State, and Law and Order* (London: Macmillan, 1978).

Hawking, Stephen, and Penrose, Roger, *The Nature of Space and Time* (Princeton, NJ: Princeton University Press, 1996).

Hayford, Casely, *Ethiopia Unbound: Studies in Race Emancipation* (London: C. M. Phillips, 1911).

Hebdige, Dick, *Subculture: The Meaning of Style* (1975; London: Routledge, 2002).

Hegel, George Wilhelm, 'The Natural Context or the Geographical Basis of World History', *Lectures on the Philosophy of World History*, trans. H. B. Nisbet, ed. Duncan Forbes (Cambridge: Cambridge University Press, 1975).

Hiro, D., *Black British, White British* (Harmondsworth: Penguin, 1972).

Hobson, John, *Imperialism: A Study* (1902; repr. London: George Allen & Unwin, 1938).

Horowitz, Sara, 'Voices for the Killing Ground', in *Voicing the Void: Muteness and Memory in Holocaust Fiction* (Albany, NY: University State of New York Press, 1997).

Horton, James Africanus Beale, *Letters on the Political Condition of the Gold Coast* (London, 1870).

Hsia, R. Po-Chia, *Trent 1475: Stories of a Ritual Murder Trial* (New Haven, Conn.: Yale University Press, 1992).

Hurston, Zora Neale, 'How It Feels to be Colored Me' (1928); repr. in *The Norton Anthology of African-American Literature*, ed. Henry Louis Gates and Nellie Y. McKay (New York: Norton, 1997).

Husserl, Edmund, *Lectures on the Phenomenology of Internal Time-Consciousness*, trans. John Brough (Dordrecht: Kluwer, 1991).

Huyssen, Andreas, *Twilight Memories: Marking Time in a Culture of Amnesia* (London: Routledge, 1995).

Ilona, Tony, *Wasafiri*, 2 (Autumn 1995), 3–9.

James, Cyril Lionel Robert, *History of Negro Revolt* (London, 1938).

John, Errol, *Moon on a Rainbow Shawl* (London: Faber & Faber, 1958).

Johnson, Lemuel, *Shakespeare in Africa (and Other Venues): Import and the Appropriation of Culture* (Trenton, NJ: Africa World Press, 1998).

Johnston, Sir Harry, *The Negro in the New World* (London: Methuen, 1910);

Juneja, Renu, *Caribbean Transactions: West Indian Culture in Literature* (London: Macmillan, 1996).

King, Bruce, *West Indian Literature* (London: Macmillan, 1995).

King, Martin Luther, *A Testament of Hope: The Essential Writings and Speeches of Martin Luther King, Jr.*, ed. James Washington (New York: Harper Collins, 1991).

Kitson, Martin, and Rotberg, Robert, *The African Diaspora: Interpretive Essays* (Cambridge, Mass.: Harvard University Press, 1976).

La Capra, Dominick, *History and Memory after Auschwitz* (Ithaca, NY: Cornell University Press, 1998).

Lawson, Steven, *Running for Freedom: Civil Rights and Black Politics* (Philadelphia: Temple University Press, 1991).

Levi, Primo, *Moments of Reprieve*, trans. Ruth Feldman (London: Michael Joseph, 1986).

MacInnes, Colin, *City of Spades* (London: Allison & Busby, 1957).

McKay, Claude, *Banjo* (London: Harper & Bros., 1929).

Marx, Karl, *Political Writings*, vol. ii, trans. Ben Fowkes and Paul Jackson (Harmondsworth: Penguin, 1973).

—— and Engels, Freidrich (1952) *Manifesto of the Communist Party* (Moscow: Progress Publishers, 1848; repr. 1952).

Mavor, William Fordyce, *History of the Dispersion of the Jews; of Modern Egypt; and of other African Nations* (London, 1802); in *Universal History: Ancient and Modern, from the Earliest Records of Time, to the General Peace of 1801*, 25 vols. (London, 1802–4).

Mbiti, John Samuel, *African Religions and Philosophy* (1969; repr. London: Heinemann, 1990).

Michaels, Anne, 'Cleopatra's Love', *Poetry Canada Review* (March 1994).

Nasta, Susheila (ed.), *Motherlands: Black Women's Writing from Africa, the Caribbean and South Asia* (London: Women's Press, 1991).

Newton, Isaac, *The Principia: Mathematical Principles of Natural Philosophy* (1687), trans. Bernard Cohen and Anne Whitman (Berkeley and Los Angeles: University of California Press, 1999).

Newton, John, *Letters to a Wife*, 2 vols. (London, 1793).

Nicholson, Stuart, *Billie Holiday* (London: Victor Gollancz, 1995).

Nkrumah, Kwame, *Neo-Colonialism: The Last Stage of Imperialism* (London: Nelson, 1965).

Okri, Ben, 'Meditation on Othello', *West Africa*, 30 March 1997, 610–19.

Osbourne, Peter, *The Politics of Time: Modernity and Avant Garde* (London: Verso, 1995).

Plato, *The Dialogues of Plato*, ed. B. Jowett, 4 vols. (Oxford Clarendon Press, 1953).

Procter, James (ed.), *Writing Black Britain, 1948-1998: An Interdisciplinary Anthology* (Manchester: Manchester University Press, 2000).

Ramdin, Ron, *Reimaging Britain: Five Hundred Years of Black and Asian History* (London: Pluto, 1999).

Ricoeur, Paul, *Time and Narrative*, trans. Kathleen McLaughlin and David Pellauer (Chicago: University of Chicago Press, 1988).

St Augustine, *The Confessions*, ed. Maria Boulding (London: Hodder & Stoughton, 1997).

Senghor, Leopold Seghar, *The Africa Reader: Independent Africa* (London: Vintage, 1970).

Smith, Lillian Eugenia, *Strange Fruit [A Novel]* (London: Cresset Press, 1945).

Spillers, Hortense, and Pryse, Marjorie (eds.), *Conjuring Black Women: Black Women, Fiction and Literary Tradition* (Bloomington, Ind.: Indiana University Press, 1985).

Walcott, Derek, *Henri Christophe: A Chronicle in Seven Sequences* (Bridgetown: Advocate Co., 1950).

—— *Midsummer* (London: Faber & Faber, 1984).

White, John, *Billie Holiday: Her Life and Times* (London: Omnibus Press, 1988).

Williams, Patrick, and Chrisman, Laura (eds.), *Colonial Discourse and Post-Colonial Theory: A Reader* (Hemel Hempstead: Harvester, 1994).

Wolfenstein, Eugene Victor, *The Victims of Democracy. Malcolm X and the Black Revolution* (Berkeley and Los Angeles: University of California Press, 1981).

Wright, Richard, *Native Son* (London: Victor Gollancz, 1940).

X, Malcolm, *Autobiography of Malcolm X*, ed. Alex Hayley (London: Hutchinson, 1965).

Index

Printed in the United Kingdom
by Lightning Source UK Ltd.
115850UKS00001B/31-108

9 780746 309568